WALKS
ON THE
MARGINS

WALKS ON THE MARGINS

A Story of Bipolar Illness

Kathy Brandt
Max Maddox

Monkshood

Published by Monkshood Press

1   3   5   7   9   10   8   6   4   2

Manufactured in the United States of America

ISBN 978-0-9891414-0-6

Library of Congress Control Number 2013905281

Cover art and design by Max Maddox ©2013

For Jessi,
and all the sisters and brothers
of those with mental illness

Contents

1

The Electric Blue Hour

Max

Fine chocolates and white wine, little soaps and body powders wrapped in satin yellow bows, a diamond accented with emeralds on a band of white gold. The Love Park fountain bursting through the city lights. A childish quartet splashing in the baby blue, exhilarated by the coming of the hour. The air was for once fresh, the flags of the avenue full as sails with the warmth of summer. Sisters of hers, brothers of mine, drifted by, the priest, the promenade.

The scene was fleeting, emptying, disappearing. She never came, and where I thought my walk had ended, it had only just begun. And so I stood. Twisting precious gems around my little finger, to my fair lady I heeded the signs. The flier on the telephone pole, in the newspaper box, the ad on the side of the bus. The arrangement of flowers in the store window, the stray cat, the draw of the cicada's pulse, the charms that fell from her bracelet.

Bent over like a real beggar, smelling like fungus and urine, I walked on the same blisters, only bigger. Gruesome, unnerving, crimson silver dollars on my Achilles heel, medallions on my walks over the horizon, marathons on the margins. On the fissures in the bricks of the lovesick, in the storm that would right everything wrong, it was for her, my paradise.

She was a promise, one that could never be made good. But a promise so great that its very mirage crippled even the strongest of wills. If I finally do recover, it will be from my undying love for her; it will be from a broken heart.

But let me start from the beginning, nearly 12 years ago now.

★

It was just before sunrise, at the electric blue hour I had come to appreciate in the week since I had given up sleeping. That early morning, George W. Bush was making one of his first appearances on TV, his image forming there before me in a virtual dance across the screen. He moved as if to music only he heard, waving his effortless wave, just to my left, just to my right, squinting over here, shaking hands where they needed to be shook.

My eyes alit on parted hair, red neckties, and baby-boomer wives, while I considered this little epicycle in the conservative political upheaval, suddenly motioning around this one individual. So far as I was concerned, the man was already president. I had told my good friend Anna it was the best course, the course we are always on, painful as it is. The conditions for a revolution would be made.

You can hardly tell the difference between a lunatic and

a young Marxist, but there is one. Actually, there are at least two: eating and sleeping. Anna was concerned enough to emphasize to me their importance. I don't think she had ever been so serious. We agreed with Karl that the "dispute over the reality or non-reality of thinking that is isolated from practice is a purely *scholastic* question." And still, against my advice, she continued to make her way to Poli Sci class, and whatever else she signed up for that semester. It had become clear that if either of us would be going anywhere, we would not be going together.

Though I'd taken some time for a little "independent study," you still might say I had a hungry mind that year. I had never been so interested in reading and my retention and focus had come together in an extraordinary way. I would have just as soon strolled through the astrophysics aisles at the library, flipping through the giant books of equations at ten pages per second, shall we say, than fidget my way through another philosophy lecture on monads.

Just a few days erstwhile, I thought to win the Nobel Peace Prize for my work some day; it seemed perfect for what I was doing. But all of that had become irrelevant. I was at a historical crossroads of sorts, one whose effect couldn't be entirely known by the legions and arbitrators of history, including its prize givers. Sometime in the night, I had made plans for the morning's activities. I had become the king of making plans then. But this one was simple.

I took one last long pull off the pipe, put it back on the arm of the chair, and left. Three cans of spray-paint and my mom's manual Minolta in my backpack, I walked down the steps into a perfect morning. It was one of those days that feels like your birthday, like you could have anything.

The songbirds from the trees lining Broad Street recoiled

around my fixation on their asymmetric cries. Down 6th Street, the bank sign flashed coded APR rates and sent out its congratulations to the recently wedded, its witty absurdities poignant, settling me into this riddle.

SEPTEMBER 08, 1999
55 F, 12.8 C
INTEREST RATES
RISE AGAIN
6.25%
CONGRATULATIONS
ON YOUR DAY
TED & SYLVIA
JONES!!!!

I rounded a familiar corner to the long red brick wall outside the entrance to the local dive bar tucked in behind Main Street. Underground and shrugging at "code," the details of which didn't make it that far inland, it was here that many of us eighteen-twenty year olds regularly spent a few nights a week guzzling pitchers of Wisconsin macro and playing violent games of foosball. It is in Iowa where these talents are best honed, and hidden potential is best found and lost over the course of a night.

My face was inches from the wall as the aerosol spread its colored mist, encircling my head and speckling my face like St. Augustine on his last ascent. For the next three and a half years, on the way to drown ourselves on a given night, my friends and I would avert our eyes from the three overlaid spellings of "GOD" in primary enamels as we tripped back down to the pub for another forgettable night. If I had only written something else, there would have been more to say.

But even on this morning my mouth was as though stitched shut, and my possessions were as my chains. Watch, wallet, and keys, and shoes disposed of, I tossed the empty cans to the asphalt of the silent alleyway, catching the eyes of another early riser, unsure whether she had just witnessed a crime.

A full day's spin of the earth, and the light fell the same way it ever had. In Grinnell, Iowa, that September, the sun stretched out across two-story buildings, lapping against the hard green leaves, washing the wind into form. At a yellow-orange daybreak, I snapped black and whites at my reflection in tinted office windows. Facsimile of the inverted horizon bent in my camera's lens, I turned its focus on all of the instances of reflection. With each snap the change in light grew more rapid until my face was overtaken from behind by the steep rays of the sun. The solitude of the early morning was slipping away; I grew embattled with the delay of what I had expected to be an outcome of sorts.

Baggy-eyed pig farmers, in it for another day, emerged from their respective holes. Something about my appearance had caught them off-guard, and they silently encouraged me to make my way out of this town of ten thousand. Along the way, I decided to continue my summer in Bodega, California, where for months last summer I lay with *Leaves of Grass*, ate blackberries, and hippie-flipped in the redwoods with my donkey neighbor on "The Ranch."

Whether I was laid out by someone headed east, the sun pouring into their windshield, my blood exploding over the corn on either side of the highway, or whether I was afforded a more elegant departure into pure enlightenment, I was willing to digress in an ongoing way, as far as my feet would take me down that two-lane.

Wind flowing through my face holes, bare feet on a yellow balance beam, I-80 to I-76 to Highway 50. The cars piled up, trailing my slow gait; even behind the wheel, courteous as Midwesterners should be, they minded their own business as they crept by on my right. I had not in fact made myself invisible as I would have had myself believe.

When will you wake up, deep thinkers, heavy drinkers, all washed-up while I do all the work of the wake? Take my maps, my unfinished projects, my rude and unmeaning poetry, and meet me here, at the corner of this checkered parachute. Clinch the tapered edge, spread tight this fabric over the cliffs of the Pacific! Snap hard this horrible nylon quilt! Lock your arthritic claw, let your skeleton smash against this shore of black rock! Keep forever the smile of the skinless jaw!

The chirp of a siren at my tail broke me free from this last plea for company, waking me from the utter loneliness of pure faith. I gathered that I was being pulled over by the local outfit, so I moved to the shoulder in the customary way. Here in the middle of nowhere, not even farmers believe in the devil anymore, and the local bookstores had long carried the latest version of the *Diagnostic and Statistical Manual.* Most of the cops know when to throw you in jail and when to take you in for a check-up.

A little Q&A nonsense, some vitals and the cold coin of a stethoscope, and the doctors found me sickly and undernourished, flighty and over determined. My friend Will showed up at the hospital and identified me as the specimen I was—by all appearances his roommate. The causes of my ailment seemingly extra-physical, I was sent to Des Moines on a narrow slip in the back of an ambulance.

I have been on a number of these rides now, whipping around corners, laying it out on expressways, wondering why we were always going so fucking fast. Fully enjoying it though, not having so much as a splinter, as I made my way to the more appropriate hospital, feeling as though I'd finally found someone to agree with my assessment of the critical situation.

Dear red suited man, what could you possibly say? I who am looking up at you, you who belted me to this cart. We who have never met are locked together in a swiftly moving box, listening like you do, eyes inside-out, wide blue open to the stream, fast babble and deep heaves, blowing my word-train into your face.

★

A flash of the fully lit day, and I was rolled through the west wing of Mercy Hospital, almost every bed without an occupant that sunny Tuesday. I told them who I was (everyone) and where I was from (everywhere), crying into my hands as a lady in white scribbled out a few notes, enough syndromes for a diagnosis.

"This must be so hard for you," she said with sad eyes.

The mere suggestion of sympathy had me feeling the exhaustion of the most intense experience of my life. I slipped into sleep on top of the cream blankets, my mind whirring around the pantomime of my advent into this new world, losing myself in the margins of my dreams, flowing into my waking life with such ease.

But no more than an hour later, I was renewed for a majestic evening. With the success of the mission and the new tomorrow, the turn of events, unified theories and the what-not, I almost didn't notice I was locked up. And quickly I found the mental hospital had any number of outlets suited to a sufferer such as myself, any combination of which could make the inside seem even better than the out. Truth be told, watching a bit of TV suited me just fine. It was really a different show altogether, slight documentary of the gods, quiet commentaries whose murmur was barely audible on QVC and made-for-TV movies.

"These are *real* diamonds folks, *just beautiful*, look at them. *Real* diamonds. And as we pan out, take in the aquamarine business-casual attire, we see Elaine is wearing a sexy and lightweight open-back dress, for just *$29.95* if you call now! *Just beautiful!*"

"It must feel like you're wearing nothing at all!" Isolate with the truth on cable, in the off-season at the house of indignities, one or two ass cracks peeking through hospital issue garb, nobody really seemed to get it.

But it wouldn't be long now. Soon enough my folks, sisters, pharmacists, not long the government, the United Nations...What design! What intricate design! Was I the first? No, no. Just another beacon of the message. I tried to explain this to an old lady in a wheelchair while we watched *Guiding Light*. She suffered from nothing more than anxiety at the precipice of the after-life. We were not so different! On the escalator we held hands.

And of course my parents were right on time; they'd had their own long trip. They looked to me for answers, answers which only led to more questions, their eyes falling on me as they never had before. They were an audience in wait. Dare I say it, they were in *awe*, watching my performance with fantastic enchantment, simply astonished. I spoke to them my art-politico, refolded my unifying theories from thin air, relaying the news, insisting it was right there in the music, trickling from the old nuthouse radio.

Even the doctors and their personnel seemed complicit in the plan. And, indeed, by them no accusations of wishful thinking were necessary. When all is said and done, every-thing takes care of itself in the emporium of perfumes. If it don't have a brand, it don't have a flavor: Christian Dior, Elizabeth Taylor. A spray for you, a spray for me, a spray for the nurses bored watching TV.

The overactive and the underactive opened wide their mouths, in rainbow colors we pinched our paper cups. At the front of the line, the meth-head like a monkey waited on his treat, pulling up the rear, the acute psychotic stood dithering with his tongue stricken stiff. Now now, there there, another dose put him back to sleep. So his saliva fell, seeping through the perforated corridors of his foam pillow, the same piece of bread as the last tenant in 12B.

2

Elopement Risk

Kathy

"Turn on the news," Max said. I flipped through the channels in an idiotic and desperate attempt to find answers, praying that it was the world that had tipped and not my son. CNN reported on Bill Clinton's upcoming meeting with his Chinese counterpart, Jiang Zemin. Wally and The Beav shot baskets in the driveway as June watched from the window, her arms elbow-deep in soapy water. But I knew this wasn't the idyllic new world my son was talking about.

I called him back, confused. "You just don't understand, Mom," he said and hung up.

It was five a.m. but I began calling—college counselors, deans, professors—anyone who might be able to tell me what was happening to my son eight hundred miles away in that tiny Iowa town. All I got were answering machines until I connected with Max's best friend and roommate, Will.

"Max was up watching TV all night," he said. "I heard him

go out the door about 5:30. I don't know what's going on. He's not acting like Max."

Max's sister, Jessi, had yet to return to Minneapolis for her fall semester at college and was the first to put a name to it—manic depression. She stared out the window on a sweet fall afternoon as she told the story of a girl in her biochemistry class last year. "She was kind of quiet and then suddenly she was keeping her roommate up all night, wandering the dorm, cutting class. Her parents took her home. When she came back the next semester, she told me she was diagnosed with bipolar disorder."

I was confused, numb, waiting for someone to shake me awake or tell me it was some great mix-up—a different Max Maddox, the misfortune of another mother.

"But she seems fine now, Mom," Jessi said hesitantly, offering priceless encouragement when it mattered most, as she always had, even as a child. Over the months and years that followed, I grasped at that straw, the one she lent me that first day.

By that afternoon, Max had been picked up by the police and taken to Mercy Psychiatric Hospital in Des Moines, and his step-dad, Ron, and I were on our way to Iowa. We headed north, past the snow-tipped Front Range to Denver, then east across the vast stretch of plains, our tires groaning down an infinite black line. Through Nebraska, the tick, tick, tick of ruined insects marked time against our windshield as combines spat a wild dust over fields of brown rubble. The sting of the decaying Midwest burned in my throat as our metal box rolled across the terrible emptiness between here and there.

Until that morning, I'd thought that Max was fine, better than fine. I thought that he'd found himself that summer, which he spent reading poetry and salmon fishing at his uncle's commune off the coast of Northern California. When I'd dropped him off at the airport just two weeks ago for his return for fall semester at Grinnell College, he didn't doubt anything. He seemed happier and more confident than ever in his twenty years. He'd been pleased about his house, an old rundown Victorian just blocks from campus, five bedrooms, four roommates.

"I've got the room in the back. It's small but I like the privacy and the light is good."

He'd learned to think about light, how it comes in the windows, fills the room, touches a canvas. Philosophy was his major but art was becoming his passion.

As the days passed, his calls home had become more intense. He'd filled every waking hour, serving on the Philosophy Department committee, "spinning records" at a party, filling a notebook with poetry, and publishing his cartoons in the school magazine. He said he'd quit drinking, become a "raw foodist," and was "shooting consistent three-pointers."

"I love art, life, you guys. Things are so intense. But," he'd added, "I have a severe case of mind-racing insomnia."

★

"Maybe we should get something to eat before we go inside," Ron suggested as we sat in the hospital parking lot, staring out the car window. Eyes glazed behind thick lenses, he'd begun to realize that he'd be taking care of me as I tried to take care of Max, developing an emotional triangle that would begin here, persisting and strengthening as the years went on. But at the moment food seemed out of the question. I had to get inside to find out how bad things really were.

The hospital door was locked. A sign above the bell read "Elopement Risk. Ring for entrance." *Elopement risk?* My father, joking about the expense of weddings for his four daughters, defined "elopement" as running away, finding a justice of the peace and a little chapel in Las Vegas. But I knew this could only be about the running away. This was lockdown, the reality of the psych ward.

We found Max near the nurses' station performing handstands, his long arms straining, muscles defined, ribs protruding, his body thinner than I ever remember.

"Matty," I whispered.

He dropped to his feet, his baggy pants settling at his hips. He smiled and wrapped his arms around us. I could feel his fleshless bones. But his substance calmed me. He took us to the lounge where patients slouched in overstuffed chairs like old party balloons. Already he knew them all. He was a light in the muted space—electric, on fire, talking nonstop about ethics and religion, math and astrology, incorporating everything around him into a mixed-up metaphysical philosophy, quickly picking up speed. He reminded us that it was September 9, 1999—9-9-99, a momentous convergence of time and events. He skirted from one person to the next, drawing them into the story.

A nurse found us there in the lounge, faces frozen on our son. He introduced himself and led us to a conference room, a windowless affair where incessant fluorescent lights buzzed like belabored wasps.

"We don't believe in hiding anything from our patients," he explained as he closed the door, "but usually family members feel more comfortable talking without their loved one in the room. Let me get right down to it. Max's symptoms are classic. He has bipolar disorder, specifically Bipolar I."

"How can you be so sure?" I asked, still grasping.

"He's manic and delusional. The other likely explanation would be drugs, and none showed up in his blood tests, except for traces of marijuana. But if I had to choose the mental illness that my kid might have," he continued, "this is the one I'd take. With the right medication, bipolar disorder is treatable. Max can do well."

I found myself wondering what doing "well" meant. Healthy, thriving? In the pink? Hale and hardy? Or better than now, better than a copper penny flattened by a train. "We need to take him home," I said.

"Max is on a seventy-two-hour hold. Court-ordered. A hearing will be scheduled to determine whether he can be released."

"Court? You must be kidding."

"It's just a formality. I'm sure the judge will release him to your care."

Ron and I were at the hospital early every morning and left late. Max spilled so many words we couldn't keep up as he drew us to the floor to help him with a puzzle. He placed the pieces on the carpet in swirls of color and told us that every work of art is perfect because it's a reflection of the artist. He said everything that happens was the perfect occurrence, and we were the perfect parents. He told us that people who are insane are keyed into higher levels of thinking and that they would teach everyone else. He seemed to understand that he was mentally ill, but to him it was all part of the wisdom bestowed on him.

Every day as we walked out of the unit, I fought against my vision of what the future held. Max was so happy in his new world and I knew that world would all fall apart.

Four days later, we left the safety of the hospital with Max and a brown paper bag filled with Depakote and Zyprexa samples, mysterious concoctions that were supposed to return our son to us. We headed back across the Midwest to Colorado, listening to Max's rap music, seeking a teeter-totter balance between his need to talk and our need for calm. He sat in the back seat, explaining the lyrics and trying to teach us "the way." We kept the car doors locked against a sudden jump.

We stopped in Council Bluffs, York, Kearney, Ogallala, Brush. Max was out of the car quickly, lighting up a Camel. Ron and I took turns standing outside bathroom doors or trying to keep track of him as he roamed the aisles at truck stops. We could easily imagine him just walking away, hitching a ride with a trucker, or vanishing into a cornfield. During the sixteen-hour drive back to Colorado, Max gave us a thorough introduction to the throes of mania and a crash course on parenting a son with manic depression.

At home my plans were simple. I'd roast chicken and heap mashed potatoes onto his plate. I'd dish up huge bowls of strawberry ice cream, brew herb teas, and heat warm milk and Max would sleep. When he woke, he would be my son again.

3

Margaritaville

Max

An old bearded psychiatrist did his best, and so he said, "These are my paintings of ducks." But our agenda was crystal clear, bound up in the *Merck Manual* that sat on his bookshelf, somewhere between Robert Bly's *Iron John* and Roger Tory Peterson's *Field Guide to Western Birds*. The very same copy of the drug manual sits on my own bookshelf as I write, and I frequently use this piece of stolen property to identify the long list of drugs that I've been prescribed over the years.

I love the feel of the book's smooth black cover, the gold embossed letters, the cut and dry attitude I associate with solid science. But not having much affinity for medicine, I felt at first unwilling to accept even the givens. It's natural to be optimistic, I think, as the onset of depression can delay for months. During my first interim of the sort, I had plenty of time and reason to start believing that I was not a sick man after all.

But quick was the rant and rattle of suicidal ideation to snuff out completely any lingering hope for a normal life. The question of how and where I could end the agony soon turned into a habit of minute-by-minute thinking, like a compulsion to open and close a door. A grim, grim man alone with his feelings about his lost youth, I withered like the fig tree that didn't produce. The ache deep in head and hinge never subsided. I woke up with it; I went to sleep with it. It was in the food; it was in the pillow bag. It spread across the carpet and covered the old bulletin board. It was on the radio, it was on the TV, the news, the terrible news, the coming war and the defeat, the defeat, the defeat. *Everywhere the defeat.*

A quick chop, slash, or hack with a blade sharpened to cut deep, fast; the cool pull of the trigger of an Arisaka once lifted by my grandfather from the chest of a "cold Jap;" a jump off the highway overpass, the tallest building in town, the edge of the Royal Gorge; radiation, cyanide, the fever of a black widow. The bends, an accidental drowning off the coast of Martinique, a plastic bag and a belt, a match and a can of gasoline.

"The breaks were cut, the parachute didn't open. Somehow the tornado found him. He had his lunch packed, he was in the middle of a drawing, he had become a daring outdoorsman." Or be more direct, and honest, try to get my family to reason with me. "Nobody wants this, let's cut our losses" or something along those lines. "I am ready to die, please don't blame yourselves."

Something had to be done. More mood stabilizers, fewer antipsychotics, a different family of anti-depressants, a new one, a proven one, an experimental one, a conservative one; avant-garde natural medicines, wild Atlantic salmon, fish oil from an eyedropper, good old Vitamin D. More activity, less activity, more exercise, more time to rest, less time alone, a little time abroad. Or go back to school, there's one down the street! Postmodern philosophy, why not? What's postmodernism? Who knows! Who cares! Anything to distract me from a depression that had become usual, even uninteresting.

I forgot what you said as you said it, Mr. Lyotard, Dr. Parsons, fellow students, doing what they could to forget I was there while my worth further depreciated at the corner desk. For my final paper I decided on some doodles and my suicide note. Offense not taken, they would have to admit how *postmodern* was my anguish, how agreeable was my desire for a more decisive and declarative nature. And on that note, I have nothing to show for my cowardice in taking control over my own life or over my own death, but it seems in natural company with my inability to write a 'final paper.'

Quit school, never leave the house, eat *Basic 4* for every meal. Go to sleep. *God, go to sleep.* Shut hard under the sharp edges of my skull, flashing red branches leaving green traces in the warm dark of my cavern, I raged for another hour of sleep until finally hypnotized into dream by the steady tick of my self-hatred, where the hand holding the chain holds no sway and the unconscious weave holds out its answers. I awoke disgraced, morning noon or night, Monday or Friday, the same lingering taste at the tip of my dry tongue, like a name whose thought made my mind blank.

★

My movements shaped the river of blue tang, flowing at arm's length around me, thousands of eyes sliding by on every side, moving through the ocean's broad blue tongue, saying something so slowly you lose focus on its saying.

Everything that falls in changes the sea forever. The giant sea turtle is a receptacle of this ancient rule. It swims never closer to one thing than another, dipping through the wide spaces between shimmering anemones and black urchins latched to the grand porous bones of the reef, grabs against the sea with her perfectly formed fins, tattooed with the patterns of refracting light bending in at her colossal shell.

Without looking back, she shot deep into the Atlantic.

Handed the Virgin Islands on a silver platter and all we had to show for ourselves was this drawn out Jimmy Buffet concert.

"Can you believe he wrote these songs right here on this island?"

"No, I could not possibly believe that." Rancid golden calf, ground chuck and cheddar sinking onstage with a gloomy electric guitar, withering under the dull-drum of his own melody, harkening the stiffs in paradise to bend in a halfway dance. Wasting away, wasting away indeed, hairy beer bellies and bloated busts, 285 kinds of flip flop and sixteen grades of suntan lotion, yet saggy old queens turned to burnt toast on the decks of floating trailers moored together at the mouth of the New World.

This, too, was a vacation spot for the adventurous. I was witness to the slow suicide of its disjointed offspring, finished with life before it had yet ended. I, too, was one of its citizens, loafing at its broken feet.

4

$100 Nikes

Kathy

Some days Max and I would talk for hours, our exchanges circling in on themselves without closure. Sometimes our talk was deeply philosophical, sometimes pragmatic. We were trying hard to make sense out of something that might never make any sense. He was a twenty- year-old kid, trying to figure out just who he was and what was real. Everything had been so clear; he'd been so confident. And what about the medication? Did it keep him from being who he really was or was it turning him back into the person he'd always been?

Watching Max suffer at home, we sought normality and structure for his days. For Max, that had always been school. So he signed up for a class in Postmodern Philosophy at Colorado College. I was encouraged by his determination. But soon Max would return in the afternoon and drop onto his bed, arm thrown over his face. Each day he struggled fiercely to block out the anxiety and feelings of incompetence. He managed to write two short papers, but by the time the final paper came he simply could not find the words. He had always been able to meet the challenge of academia. After all, he'd been doing the assignment since the first grade. But on the last day of class he met with the dean of students and for the first time admitted his illness to a stranger, who signed off on an incomplete.

Max dropped deeper and deeper into depression. We made sure he was never left in the house alone. I often found him in his room, curled in on himself, eyes squeezed shut. I'd sit on the edge of his mattress, rubbing his back as I had when he was little and feared the green trolls that hid beneath his bed. I told him again and again that this nightmare would also end. But sometimes I went down to the basement, examining the floor joists to see whether a rope could be strung around one of the beams. I pulled on the pipes in the ceiling to see if they would hold a person's weight. I hated that basement, its cold cement walls sloughing off damp blackened concrete.

Max's psychiatrist told us to be aware that antidepressants could throw Max back into mania. "Take him on the sailing trip you've planned. If he feels anxious and agitated, he should decrease the Wellbutrin; if he gets even more depressed, increase it. Just go."

I don't think Max really wanted to make the trip, but then there was little he could bring himself to want or do, and Ron and I thought a little tropical paradise would do all three of us some good. There were few places I'd rather be than anchored in the aquamarine water of a quiet harbor, breathing the fresh salty air and getting a little respite. I hoped Max could find some deliverance in the calmness of the sea too.

So we flew to the British Virgin Islands and headed across the Anegada Passage, 7500 feet deep, open to unpredictable Atlantic swells and trade winds that would push us away from our destination, Saint Martin, 81 miles away. By the time night fell, we had left the sight of land and were absorbed in the vast ocean where the only lights shown from our bow and the distant ships that twinkled on the dark horizon.

In the blackest part of the night, we couldn't tell where the sea ended and the sky began. The force of the wind rattled the mast and sculpted our sail into a crescent moon. We grew accustomed to the rhythm, bow pitching down into a trough, then up to the crest. We were well prepared. We wore scopolamine patches behind our ears to prevent seasickness and life jackets with strobe lights that activate on contact with the water.

Every sailor's nightmare is to fall overboard into the black sea and disappear behind the swells as the boat glides away. At watch on deck alone, fear could run unchecked if I let it. I wanted my mind empty, but the questions tangled as the waves lapped against the hull.

★

Divorce wasn't something I thought would happen to me. My parents had stayed together until the day they died, my brother, sisters—all in their marriages, good or not. I was one of five kids, growing up in the 50s and 60s in a small town in Illinois, attending mass every Sunday. Even though I'd left Catholicism behind when I left home, it sticks to your gut. Catholics don't divorce.

My marriage to Nolan, Max's dad, hadn't made it four years. Jessi was not even two. Max still curled in my belly, just weeks from being born. Nolan never fought for custody, whether because he knew he'd never get the kids or because he didn't want them, I never knew. But suddenly, I found myself a single mom at thirty-two.

Child support came in the form of returned checks marked "insufficient funds," and I scrambled to make ends meet. I found an apartment in Colorado Springs that flooded every time it rained, and I drove an old blue Chevy station wagon that my brother sold to me for $1.00. Just to get it started, I had to prop a pencil in the carburetor.

I was determined that the kids not suffer from a one-parent household. I would love them enough for two. I would convince them they were secure and that I would never leave them. I carried them in slings and backpacks, and held their hands. They ran through the sprinkler, splashed in a plastic wading pool, dug in the sandbox, and made snowmen. They wore silly pointed birthday hats and blew out pink and green candles. I fixed mac and cheese, peas, and mashed potatoes. They wore cowboy hats and carved pumpkins, dressed as princesses, monsters, witches, and Indians, and I decorated their bedroom door with their drawings of spiders and ghosts.

Eventually, I found a little house I could hardly afford to rent in a neighborhood of tightly gathered homes separated by short fences. It wasn't the kind of house in which I had envisioned raising my kids, not like the one where I'd grown up, surrounded by forests and fields where we could run forever. I wasn't really sure that kind of idyllic neighborhood existed anymore. But the house had a big back yard and I found a swing set at a garage sale.

At night, the kids in bed, I would sit at the kitchen table crying at my failure. I was shocked at being a divorced woman. My return to school was as much about regaining some self-esteem as it was about getting a degree. I studied at night or as the kids played. When I was in class, they attended the college childcare center. I survived on grant money and college loans and the tutoring I did as part of a work-study program. The kids didn't need a lot yet—clothes always came their way from grandparents, the rest from yard sales. But I barely managed rent and groceries, and ran up my bill at daycare. I was always behind and cutting corners.

Jessi watched over her brother, comforted him when he cried, decorated his hair with colorful plastic barrettes, helped him with his buttons, and spun circles in celebration when he took his first step. They found ways to be secure--Jessi with her Raggedy Ann wrapped in her arms, Max dragging a Winnie the Pooh pillow behind him. We were a tightly knit family of three and I couldn't have loved them more. There wasn't anything I wouldn't do to keep them safe and happy.

Max was four and Jessi six when I finished my Master's degree and started teaching. I always had a stack of papers that needed to be graded, but I scheduled all my classes for three days a week and did all my grading and class preparation at home. All too soon, Jessi skipped down the sidewalk to start kindergarten and then Max followed.

I never said much to the kids about Nolan and he made little effort to see them. Max didn't really know his dad, having been born after we split up. When his father did visit, Max was confused and reluctant. Later, I realized I should have explained in ways that little kids would understand why we'd divorced, encouraged them to talk about their feelings. But I was fine with his absence. I didn't want the kids torn between two houses, different rooms, different parents, not knowing where they belonged. I guess I didn't want Jessi and

Max to be kids of divorce. As they got older, they visited him for a couple of weeks during the summer. But the truth is that they grew up without their father and I fear that left a big hole in Max's heart.

Though I'd had no desire to remarry, the moment Ron showed up for our first date wearing an ugly striped tank top, looking like an academic California hippie and rather nerdish, I knew my plans would probably change. We married when Max was six and Jessi eight. Ron's daughter, Ingrid, was eleven and his son, Quinn, fourteen. I had just begun teaching writing at the University of Colorado and Ron was in his eighteenth year teaching biology at Colorado College. We lived in a rambling old Victorian on a wide tree-lined avenue with the small brick elementary school just across the street. Every day Ron and I worked hard to ensure this new family of six would succeed.

Summers, we packed tents, sleeping bags, camp stove, the canoe, and our yellow lab and headed into the Colorado Mountains. Or we went south to the Great Sand Dunes so the kids could touch the magic of windswept sand piled for miles through the valley of the Sangre de Christos. We waded in the pulsing river that skirted the edges of the dunes. Always we made the climb to the top of the highest one, where we admired the six sets of footprints that led up to where we sat. We'd watch the light cast a golden glow onto the sand before it disappeared on the horizon. Then the kids would run and tumble down the dune and we'd roast marshmallows over an open fire.

Still there was plenty of tension--deep sighs when the wrong parent reminded one of the kids about a chore, a constant undertone of resentment made worse when tensions were high. We went to family therapy, seeking help through the minefield. We worried about Ingrid and Quinn who had lost their mother before Ron and I married and about Jessi's angst at her mostly missing father.

Sometimes I thought the only one who was untouched was Max. He'd sit in those sessions, his legs dangling over the edge of the chair, quiet and a little confused about why we were talking to this stranger about our family. Thinking back, I wonder whether he was the one most affected and confused about his absent father and the dynamics of the blended family. He was so quiet; it was hard to know just how he was doing.

He was a good kid, rarely in trouble. He had an affinity for baseball, bow ties, and newsboy hats. He practiced viola, was the pitcher on his Little League team, played Demetrius in his fifth grade performance of "The Taming of the Shrew," elegant in purple velvet. But I felt like I had to slip a lucky charm into his pocket when he stepped out the door, worried that he might daydream himself right into the path of a Mack truck.

Like all his friends, he succumbed to the fashion that dictated his desire for $100 Nike shoes with soles that bounced on air, and he saved his allowance for months until he had enough to buy a pair. When he was seven, I brought a pound dog home, a big, white lab mix that became mostly Max's dog. She slept in his bed and he was quick to forgive her when she chewed up his favorite toy.

He collected baseball cards and comic books and romanced the redhead who lived on the corner when he was ten. At thirteen, his jeans were always too short, his hair too long, and his music too loud. At sixteen he struggled with the flower he pinned to his date's red dress then puttered to the prom in our rusted Chevy van. He graduated from the

International Baccalaureate Program at his high school then he went to college, where at twenty, he tightroped on a narrow yellow line down an Iowa highway.

★

As I sat alone on the boat deck thinking through the past, Max came up to keep me company. We sat side-by-side, our whispers sweeping across each other's faces and tumbling into the sea. Spray dusted our lips and salted our tongues. We scooped up a flying fish that landed on the deck back into the water, and for a moment I saw Max as he had always been, forgetful in his enchantment with the world.

The night lifted, turning the sea gunmetal, then indigo as the sun blasted across the water. Soon the arc of the harbor and a swath of sand emerged off the bow. Houses clung to the side of the hill like a herd of goats, palm trees were scattered up the beach on an island that was nothing if not charming. Ron and Max brought in the sails, and as the boat stopped, I dropped the anchor onto the sandy bottom, holding us in the quiet water.

We passed unmarked days, watching for mountain ranges hidden just beneath the surface of the water. As we hopscotched down the east coast of St. Martin to Tintamarre, Oyster Pond, and Ile Fourchue, I kept hoping for some signs that Max's depression was lifting. The change was slow—the fleeting smile behind his snorkeling mask when he spotted a hawksbill turtle, a chuckle when he was nipped by a sergeant major protecting its eggs.

In the heat of the afternoon, he stretched his long body out on the salon bench and read an old copy of *The Dharma Bums*. He was tanned, bearded, nose sunburned, hair bleached and tangled, old shorts wrinkled and stained. He still seemed so far away, but I could see he was on his way back to us.

5

Pretty in Pink

Max

Apartment D at "The Brande" was one of the living spaces most sought after by Grinnell students. Two blocks from campus, it had a rare touch of class for the area. Standing alone among empty lots in a small prairie, it must have been the last survivor of a block fire. It had space enough for a dinner party and was filled with furniture and kitchen goods from the former tenant, who was nice enough to sublet the place to me at the last minute.

I'm not sure I remember deciding to continue my "college career." I suppose I must have weighed some other options. Go to trade school, live in my parents' basement for the rest of my life. Move far far away, take up a life on the road, join the circus or start a cult. But you break your leg, and suddenly baseball seems like the most important thing in the world; and so you limp around, pacing behind the backstop.

There is something about stacking your books on someone else's shelf, sleeping on someone else's bed, eating off someone else's fork, that will make you feel like a guest in your own life. Never had I felt so dissociated from what should have been nothing more than the new facts of life. Among these were the details of my affliction, coming piecemeal from university presses coast to coast. Furnished with familiar and intimate anecdotes like my own, my condition apparently came with a design, a dysfunctional *type*. From the professionals I learned how to apply revisionist words like "grandiosity" and "delusion" with a tight cheek. It was actually a painful process, but if I was a fool, I wanted to know the truth.

My first days back at school, I was determined to put all my effort into academics, where I could set my smeared mind to the test. I wasn't likely to find any clues to my existential worth from my Philosophy of Language class, but it seemed to me that if I could make any sense out of the equations of Quine, I would have firmly placed myself on the side of the "rational." Whether I cared about the ambiguity of belief through the lens of symbolic logic or not, at least I could say, well, "I can do whatever you can do," and, more importantly, "I can do what I did before," an assumption for which I was very hungry to provide evidence.

The clinical perspective, it turned out, has a long and sordid history. Hippocrates claimed the manic temperament was due to an excess of the most uncharitable of the four humours. Indeed we have been considered phlegmatic for many centuries. Drooling brain matter deluding and confounding us, we wipe and wipe but to no effect, living at the edge of the sneeze. As for the other three sweetly scented humours, I had only recently felt like I would blow out my brains through the tissue folded over the bowl of blood, piss, and shit, sending what was left of my disaster splattering all over my borrowed furniture.

So maybe I was rushing things; by the end of the first week I had just begun to ascertain the complexity of my return. I had developed a nasty stutter with the girls, and I couldn't help but seem overcritical. *And I was sorry.* Really I was. I wasn't sure if it was for how I was before, or how I was after. But there was all the reason in the world to be suspicious of me. I was the worst kind of turncoat. I mean, you can't go around saying the end is near and then take extra credits just to graduate on time.

"I thought you quit school, wasn't that part of the point?" An old acquaintance had too many drinks and paralyzed me with a hug as she pressed her breast against the cave that was my chest, finding I never regained much of that weight. I could only imagine how slight I felt, how unlikely. As our ears brushed each other, I wondered if I had crossed or offended her in the past, for which I have now finally paid, a series of deliberate interruptions in history class, maybe as simple as that, or just a smugness that was enough to call for a heavy-handed punishment.

"Will that tremor eventually subside?"

"I'm not afraid," I would explain, as my eyes darted toward the door, "just a bit over-excited, possibly over-medicated."

"I'm sorry this had to happen to you," she couldn't help saying, with a look I can only assume was supposed to indicate sympathy but came off as crazed bewilderment, while her eyes kept asking me, "Are you still there?"

"Yes... no...thank you...I mean, I'm fine, everything is fine," by which I meant, "Did this really have to happen to me? Because of the wheels of causality or some sadistic plan?" *Oh God, I think she's going to hug me again.*

"If you ever need anything…" Like what? A fresh pair of socks? A snack? The cold hard shoulder of a stranger to wet with my pathological tears?

"Thank you, that means a lot to me." It meant, for instance, that I really should have given college a little more critical consideration and that the situation was probably as bad as I thought. It meant, somehow, that we were both doomed in an embrace with nothing to commit us to life or each other but a few scraps of some brat pack movie scripts, *Pretty in Pink*, or something like that.

But I suppose this was never about everyone else. It was just so obviously not their problem. I didn't have a gift for basketball, and I had no idea how to start a revolution. (I only made it through the first two classes of 20th-Century Latin American History.) I could only assume these were points of contention with my old roommate Will, a history major, when he looked at me like I had a lot to learn.

There was nothing more apparent than that, and I couldn't help but think that my poor retention of names and dates would set me forever behind. I had mastered dwelling on my deficits, a well-formed habit that made me difficult to be around, even for myself. Especially for myself. After all, there is no shame equal to that of a false prophet. And like I said, I could only figure that I had been thus portrayed; nobody was so bold as to confront me with the fact. It just seemed that everyone was looking just to my right, or just to my left, sighing, "You'll be fine."

Like the seeds of a dandelion whirling in the wind, the news had spread, or so I assumed. After all, I carry it with me to this day, this little green stalk. Some of my acquaintances missed the whole thing, but somehow they didn't. Dear friends returned from semesters abroad already having gotten the general picture in few confusing emails.

"Sarah! How was your semester abroad? Did you struggle with the language?"

"London was great, Max."

God, why do you look so much older? How long have I been gone? We were best friends, weren't we? Staring up the skirt of the redwood giants, two white clovers resting on our tongues, skinny ass running butt-naked into the waves, crude even to the gigantic setting sun. What carelessness! Why does it seem so long ago now, like another life even? Does it to you? And now it seems we have nothing to talk about at all. How could that be, with everything that's happened? Lifetimes have passed us by!

"Max, are you okay? I mean, *are you?*"

"I'm just getting... adjusted."

So I edged away a little at a time, toward the desk, the pencil, the cat, the stove, from what appeared, after all, to be a social crisis, and began nursing my private projects with a touch of bitterness. But maybe this was always the way things were. I had always kept to myself, gazed out the window a little too long. I understood that Kant never left the block he lived on, never once crossed the street. And I wasn't sure my voice hadn't always been a little tortured on the way out, it had always taken me a little longer to turn the page.

With time, the whole idea of my illness started to become nauseating, if it wasn't in the first place, like I had given a speech and forgotten to put on my clothes, or I got caught shitting my pants doing pull-ups in gym. And from what I understood, I didn't *really* go off the deep end. It could have even been explained by an inflated sense of humor from an excess of summer indulgences, or what the experts call "an epiphany." But all I could go on was the feeling that if the problem began in the horizon of my mind, its solution would be found there too, if there was one to be found at all. And the future had never seemed so daunting. By themselves, the accomplishments I had recently claimed to have achieved could take ten lifetimes. And God knows everyone would have relaxed a bit if I found something else to read, a little time to paint.

It's true, what they say, that people forget fast. We only have room in our minds for the most recent glints of the people on the fringes of our lives. Even someone dear to us will take us by great surprise and then seem mundane to us moments later. The language of the unexplained descends, and puts to sleep our judgments until next time. Self-perceptions, too, proved to be scraped together over the last couple of weeks.

"Oh good," was all I could say, as another spell of hog vapor descended upon campus and erased all traces and eventually all reminders of my odoriferous genes, that eye-watering smell of bleach. By spring it was clear. Nobody really gave a shit. And one way or another I came to expect a certain pattern in my life, as though I identified some small blip in an otherwise predictable curve in life's typical enjoyments and disappointments.

I went to class, did my homework. I raised my hand slightly (just enough), I wrote my Spinoza papers in the high European style. I ate dried out chicken-patty parmesan and drowned my fruity pebbles in strawberry milk. I enjoyed the company of friends again, I could take a joke. I got an unexpected hard-on in ancient philosophy during my presentation on Heraclitus, or I was flat passed out on the lounge couch with my face framed in a beer stain. Months went by and I began to wonder how anyone could've called me sick, or if anyone ever really had.

Maybe this is, after all, just another coming of age story. It could be just that lame, you can't count it out. But in the back of my mind I held steadfast the assumption that this was not just an imbalance in brain chemistry that had befallen me. Otherwise my life really had been stolen. If my friends, family, and doctors didn't understand that, I'm not sure I could have explained it. But you know, it didn't really matter. It made no difference at all.

6

Yo-Yo

Kathy

Remnants of Max's things lay on the floor in his room—an orange yo-yo, a plastic basketball hoop, a pair of socks, holes in the toes, a framed self-portrait he left for me on his dresser. Drawn with charcoal, his face is edged in chaotic black scribbles, his eyes intense, nearly hidden in the shadow of his brow. Nose straight, lips soft. There is a wild, gentleness to it. I often wandered into his room during the day, looking for some kind of reassurance.

Just days ago, Max and I had driven back to Grinnell in our enormous Chevy Suburban packed with the stuff he considered vital, one of which was a four-by-six foot canvas, his painting of a nude man crouching, surrounded by deep oranges and reds. It was getting dark when we started across the Nebraska wind-swept stretch of I-80. NPR reported that George W. Bush was somewhere up ahead in Iowa, but it was just background noise. I was focused on the rattling and banging of the canvas tied to the roof, worried that the man up there was ready to fly away. I imagined him landing on the hood of the car behind us and smashing through its windshield, the car swerving, hitting the ditch, and rolling.

We pulled over. Coatless, gloveless, the icy wind turning our fingers stiff, we hefted the canvas off the roof. I shoved my hands in my pockets and hovered as Max proceeded to cut the canvas right out of its frame, which apparently was all he'd valued about the object of my adoration. I protested as he folded the man into a stiff pile of orange and red and stomped him flat. I'd grown a motherly attachment to it in the same way I'm attached to everything the kids have ever created. But that night we drove away, leaving the man crushed on the side of the road under a no passing sign. *Fine.* Clearly I needed to learn to let some things go.

The next morning we found ourselves standing in Cunningham's Drugstore in Grinnell, surrounded by a pack of Secret Service, political aides, local cops, TV cameras, body-pierced students, and farmers in bib-overalls. George Bush was campaigning for votes in the Iowa primaries. "Nice to see you," he said and shook hands as he made his way through the crowd. Once meeting a presidential candidate in a drugstore in the middle of nowhere surrounded by this motley crew would have seemed preposterous. But I'd begun to realize that it was all relative.

And indeed I knew nothing would be the same again. I just didn't know how the illness would shape that change. I was afraid for my son and what he would face in the next years. And me? I'd already become more insular and remote. World events seemed unimportant; watching the news a matter of habit. None of it touched me. I was unwilling and unable to either sympathize with others hurt or rejoice in their successes. And sad movies were never quite sad enough to make me cry anymore.

Desperate for guidance, I sought a connection with other parents with bipolar children. I called a friend of a friend, whose son had been diagnosed going on two years. But she was immediately driven to tears and sought support from me instead. She was devastated that her son had quit Boston College and was taking community college classes piecemeal while living at home. She was despondent over the life she saw ahead for her son. I listened, speechless, praying I would not be her two years from now— devastated, hopeless, and crying to a total stranger.

I questioned whether I was wrong to support Max's decision to return to school. I feared he might be unable to meet the challenges there. But I was incapable of lowering my expectations or imagining Max should lower his. I'd read enough to know that many people with bipolar disorder can live full and fruitful lives. Many are highly successful in a traditional sense—they become doctors, lawyers, millionaires, the great artists and poets.

I'd never had those kinds of ambitions for my kids. I just wanted Max to be happy and successful in his own right. However, his self-confidence was shot and he dreaded facing the friends and faculty who witnessed his decline. Still, I thought he was right to continue in the direction he'd been headed last fall.

Looking for answers and guidance, Ron and I decided to try a family support group focused on bipolar disorder. We listened to one story after another about failed meds, noncompliance, and hospitalization. Mostly we heard the rant of one man.

"His wife is a bitch!" he said, referring to his friend's bipolar wife. "Christ, she's propositioned most of the men in their neighborhood. She drives like a maniac with the kids in the car. She's bounced checks all over town. He should just leave her."

"It's not Mandy," her husband said. "It's not her fault. She's sick." He obviously wanted to believe that the woman who resided inside the illness would find her way back out. I wanted to believe that he would stick by his wife.

"Bull. She's a whore, Jim. Accept it."

This was not a place I wanted to be. I needed reason, information, and real support for what we were going through. And I desperately needed hope, someone who could tell me that it would be okay. I was afraid there wasn't a living soul willing to tell me that. But I told myself that those who hoped weren't at this particular support group and that I could find them somewhere else, wherever that was.

★

There were no X-rays or blood tests; MRI's or CAT scans to verify Max's illness. The *DSM IV, The Diagnostic and Statistical Manual of Mental Disorders*, offered the only standardized information.

Mania—persistently elevated, expansive, or irritable mood, inflated self-esteem or grandiosity, decreased need for sleep, pressure of speech, flight of ideas, distractibility, increased involvement in goal-directed activities, excessive involvement in pleasurable activities with a high potential for painful consequences.

Depression—a lack of interest or pleasure in any activities; decreased energy; feelings of worthlessness or guilt; difficulty thinking, concentrating, or making decisions; negative self-worth, preoccupations with one's failures; impaired thinking and concentration, memory difficulties. Inability to function in intellectually demanding pursuits, focus on death and suicide, the desire to give up in the face of perceived insurmountable obstacles, an intense desire to end the excruciatingly emotional pain that seems never-ending.

Max is among 5.7 million adult Americans who are affected, according to the National Institute of Mental Health (NIMH). The median age of onset is 25, though it can begin in childhood or as late as the 40's and 50's. Those with bipolar disorder are expected to have a 9.2-year reduction in life span, and as many as one in five dies from suicide (NIMH). The World Health Organization reports that bipolar disorder is the sixth leading cause of disability in the world.

I remember the social worker at Mercy Hospital who told me that Max could be "fine." Psychiatrists explained "fine" in more precise terms. The illness is episodic and recurrent and there is no cure. On average, an individual will have eight to ten episodes in a lifetime, and the more episodes one has, the more likely there will be future episodes. Over half of those with bipolar disorder are unable to maintain wellness for long periods, and episodes interfere with jobs and relationships. Bipolar disorder has the highest rate of attempted suicides of any psychiatric illness.

But statistics are just cold data without consideration for individual differences. I looked for hope in stories of personal experience with the illness, which led me to Kay Jamison's book *An Unquiet Mind*, a memoir that most bipolar families find in their hands sooner or later. A professor of psychiatry at Johns Hopkins University and an expert on manic-depression, Jamison writes about her own struggle, breaking the years of silence resulting from the overwhelming stigma attached to the disorder. Her book chronicles her escalating episodes of elation followed by depression and her attempted suicide.

Jamison attributed her success to family support, good treatment, and Lithium. So in my mind, it followed that Max could be healthy and successful too. But I wanted a psychiatrist on the order of Jamison's, whom she said saved her life. At this point, Max's treatment felt piecemeal and fleeting. A couple of days in the hospital in Des Moines, a few more in Colorado Springs, and a release plan that said nothing more than "see your doctor." I envied the fact that skilled professionals surrounded Jamison. Still it took her years to get a grip on her illness.

No one knows all the factors that lead to bipolar disorder, though nearly everyone agrees that it runs in families. The potential to have a mood disorder is genetic, and investigators search for the offending nucleotides. Bipolar disorder is considered neurochemical in nature, involving neurotransmitters like serotonin and norepinephrine. Researchers hypothesize that a stressor can bring on the illness in those who are predisposed, and there seems to be nothing predictable about when or even if it will strike. For many, onset occurs in the early twenties when one leaves the security of home and meets the demands of college or a job. It may be brought on by abuse of alcohol and drugs or by hormonal changes.

All these stressors had touched Max. Grinnell was academically very challenging and he'd put a lot of pressure on himself to succeed. In spite of the demands there, students weren't strangers to the typical college benders. Many experimented with cocaine, magic mushrooms, and whatever else they could get their hands on. But most of these college kids didn't develop bipolar disorder. Perhaps the stress, the alcohol, or the drugs were the triggers for Max's first episode but they weren't the cause.

I never once considered hiding Max's illness from my friends or family and I was taken aback by the taboos surrounding mental illness. I tried to swallow my anger and explain the realities of bipolar disorder as I understood them. But I seemed only to remind my acquaintances of those frightening unknowns in the human psyche.

Psychiatric illness was stigmatized wherever I looked—on the news, in novels and movies. A Harry Potter character is characterized as mad and dangerous. Jim Carrey's character defecates on a neighbor's lawn and his girlfriend explains, "He's a schizoid."

On the other hand, mainstream cinema has managed to do better with *A Beautiful Mind*, the story of Nobel Prize winning scientist John Nash, his difficult struggle with schizophrenia, and the important role his wife played in getting him through it. Many with bipolar disorder succeed in spite of their illness--Winston Churchill, Teddy Roosevelt, Ted Turner, Robin Williams. The illness itself is often credited for bestowing the drive required to accomplish great feats.

I've often wondered whether the saints of the past would be labeled psychotic today, or if delusions lead to insights about a world others can't access. Or maybe, as Max claims, those who hear voices have antennae that reach into the cosmos. But what I did know was that when Max was manic and psychotic, he left his family, his friends, his passions, his life, behind. I didn't want him to walk through that door again. Unfortunately, if statistics had anything to do with it, he would.

7

Paradise City

Max

"You're Crazy," screamed a girl, who had been watching me thrash around at the Phantom 45 show.

I was, indeed, dancing like a maniac. Even for the Chicago rave scene, I was a little out of control. And Josh was all amped up. I swore I saw him tip back the vile of acid in the back seat of the car, but he could still DJ after all. When we got to his apartment, I kept trying to put Elective Surgery back on the turntable. He pulled me aside, twirling through his samples like a Viking falling upon a virgin over the smell of fresh bread. I closed my eyes. Everywhere were the patterns, the light.

I made disappear one more mound of white powder on a tiny spoon, without asking if it was Mali or just coke. No coffee, no toast; there was no getting out the hair of the dog. I got into my car and lay my arms over the top of the steering wheel. *Was I supposed to go back to school today, or tomorrow?*

Or was it yesterday? I was really in no condition to drive anyway, and there was plenty of time to get back to the books.

I'm afraid I had passed the point of no return in this labyrinth of ten thousand acres. But what a gorgeous day it was. I spent it cruising around town, gradually emptying my bank account. I bought some new shoes and some records for the record player I didn't have. No plans, really, waxing poetic in my cerulean car, writing down some of the more important thoughts in my sketchbook, hooked by my thumbs to the steering wheel, clothes dumped in my trunk.

Time passed me, just feeling, well, fresh, in my big baggy chinos and brand new Etnies, spinning my wheels two nights sleepless, all but forgetting who I was, just drifting on Cloud 9 in the windy city. Something had been set up, I didn't know what, just that I belonged here, with the White Sox and something about my family roots, the Great Lakes, my future, and so on, until I started to put together a picture of that which I will now speak.

★

Two Hispanic men asked me for a ride at the gas station. The crack dealers took no precautions, puffing on their dirty little glass pipe in the back seat.

"Please don't smoke crack in my car."

They did anyway, but I didn't care. These were really great guys. We stopped for some forties and cruised the barrio, N.W.A. in the tape deck, speakers rattling proper. It took some work to persuade the two that it would be cool if we dropped in unannounced at Josh's later that night, despite the generation gaps at hand, gang affiliations, my condition, you know, and the fact I didn't know my friend's address and wasn't from Chicago in the first place. But I was very eager and wouldn't contain my anticipation.

"You guys will be perfect. All the equipment is there. And you should see this sampler. You guys should ease up on that shit till we get there. I'm talkin' *Peruvian* baby."

They insisted on coming up with a little cash, feeling it impolite to show up at a coke party with no money. So we zigzagged around, parking here and there, where one peddled a dime or two while the other hung out in the car with me.

"No seriously, it's all I think about anymore."

"Yeaaaahhh Maaaaaan, move to Chicaaaago."

We were lost for what seemed like hours, but I didn't falter. "Trust me," I said, "they'll be up all night."

I rang the bell a fifth time, put my thumb on the peephole, knocked again. The door cracked open and I let myself in, my two compatriots politely introducing themselves as we took up the floor in front of the small crowd mellowed out on the couches, suddenly taken aback, me of course a little frazzled with two strung-out Latino strangers, tears tattooed at the corners of their eyes, one in his forties and one pushing sixty, the latter of whom I had taken to calling Papi.

"You act like this is some kind of heist!" Mood ruined, the shock of our entrance indelicate, without a shake of the hand or other such etiquette, at light speed I began my speech, pieced from my notes for utopia and pulled from the weave like it wasn't even some heavy shit. *Tell me this is happening to you.*

Nothing but an old daydream it seemed. From the couches they exchanged looks, blinking in disbelief at my dismal stage, where a single spot light on the stairway landed upon me as I screamed. What could they say, it was late, they were tired and in no mood for an over-enthusiastic lecture. Anyway, they were just leaving and, well, mental illness and parties never did mix.

No, not at all. But I held their audience regardless, until I was finally set free by Papi's voice, soft and easy so as not to break a fragile thing.

"Max, Max, let's get going."

And so we did, Papi driving us away into the blue saturated city, blaring Outkast's "So Fresh and So Clean," suddenly crystal-clear in the blown-out speakers of my beat-up car radio. Ice-cold the scenery passed, my shepherds silent as they carried me through the billows of restitution, just as though they had something finally to do with their lives.

"Where should we take you Max?"

"California" said one side of my mouth; "Israel" said the other.

★

Papi drove us to his friend's house. Our host, a stick figure with a mustache, closed the shades. "You know I don't want that," I said, passing up my turn in the crack rotation. At this point, though, it wasn't cool not to "take part," so Papi handed me a five dollar bill and gave me directions to the tienda for a pack of cigarettes. The last words he said to me were, "don't get lost."

But feeling my car was in good hands at the time, I was glad enough to be up early and missing in a city I had never really gotten to see with any intimacy. Twenty-two stops to Forest Park, lost in the revelry of a new epoch, visions flowing nonchalant as into waking sleep I drifted. Swift in a metal womb, the paradise city above perfectly imagined, dicing through the tunnel I landed back in the middle of the Loop unaware. I ascended the stairs into the slow pace of downtown Chicago early on a Saturday morning.

The city was mine. Giant cranes, attached to the sides of buildings, moved their hooks clockwise overhead, sweeping me from one corner to the other. Jackhammers ricocheted their sound, the diminishing echo flickering through the chamber of skyscrapers, like a boomerang snapping against the slate faces. It's thus I walked the Chicago ways, crossing over each of the bridges and back again, the canal sparkling in the morning sun, the warm shadows skirting the riverbed, the fluorescent green of budding lawns glowing by its side.

Lids half-open I paid no mind to traffic lights as I wound through downtown, slow movement of mind, rolling darkened eye, steps deliberate, perfect. I worked my way south on Clark and then west across Roosevelt, air around an over-man like a Tintoretto diviner, hooking the city on the long bridge as into Greektown I fell. The pious and keen had brightened their eyes, open so wide they turned color in the sun and the blue sky, like circles of water, they saw what I saw coming, how could they not? They needed only look around. Colossal balloons taut with air from a thousand lungs sleepily bounced through the streets, the shape of the pile of stones shifting under the feet of Chicago's citizenry.

In the end it was business as usual. Two miles west from downtown, the city slowly imploded around its shallow frame, runoff down its broken seams at wrong-turns and places better not gone. The noon hour wore on and the spring clouds opened and shut the light on the broken concrete, falling away over half-wrecked buildings, rubble strewn over ruptured lots, hood dwellers barely giving a second look at another wired white boy.

In the still electric air, the sun slid beneath a satin graphite carpet, dark gray hooks dipped toward the horizon. Arms bent, shoes off, I sent doves up to the sky in a swirl as the sun broke once more, splashing the icon on a Baptist black velvet canvas, falling to my knees I grasped for this dream coming to me *so slow*, leaving me to doubt.

"Are you okay?" Four teenagers wondered why I was bawling and curled up in the dirt among discarded drug paraphernalia.

"I NEED AN ORANGE," as in vitamin C and citrus fruit, lifted from Cezanne's bowl, the shape of release from the great weight of my role. But of course this misadventure had not befallen us all, which may have been all that ever mattered, and off they went with something to consider between them.

They would call me crazy, assuredly they had done so already. The difference I guess was that something within them remembered that God does not like to offer proof precisely when it's asked of Him. Or then again perhaps they simply knew the master plan better than I, which I couldn't now distinguish from my own.

I imagined they would bring *the others*. But so late were they to arrive, *too slow*, the sun was again eclipsed. Barefoot over broken glass, now a broken zipper, now a dog tag, now the orange marble in my pocket, too clean, I couldn't believe it, the sign of triumph was a tiny kachina made of three colors of bead. The rain began to fall as slipping to sleep I strode heavily soaked to Chicago Avenue, lit up like a movie set doubled over the streets in red letters and blue tubes melting in the backdrop of the eye of the storm.

"How did you get here?" I asked a young couple, who were nice enough to buy me a ginger ale at the 7-11.

"We live here," they said, at the entrance to their apartment building. I thought to ask them along, it seemed they could use a little fun, but they were nervous, probably feeling like they had been nice enough and sensing I was a bit "confused." Just like everyone I knew in the third dimension, to them nobody ever stepped in or out. They probably figured they existed in the only of all possible worlds.

Tragic. I must have been deceased to my family; they would never find my body. But I was determined, the portico to this world having disappeared behind me, to accept the way things were, learn the new facts of life. I pondered the landscape of my immediate and more distant futures as I loitered around the avenue. Figure the protocol, network with other over-achievers, find an entry level position with the mafia. I never doubted myself.

Envisioning black toys and custom belt buckle insignia, it was the sweep of spotlights across the sky to the east that restored promise to my enterprise. *There, there, that's where it will all go down.* Just a man, just a man, thinks he's a bat, really a basket case moving with a certain sweep, ciphers moving into place along his swift path through the concrete maze, sneaky on his way to his own surprise party. I laughed through my nose as I fled through the dark, and like a musical score my think-train brought me to the entrance of the hall.

"Welcome, Max, we've been expecting you," or so I pondered, sure of myself. I supposed I'd be on the upper deck, or no, I'd be on the dance floor, yes, slowly they'd realize I was the wizard. They would already know my work.

"Can I help you?" A security guard interrupted my whispers into the lobby.

"I thought I could lend a hand," I heard faint music, "or can I just go ahead in?" I handed over my expired driver's license, then spun around the foyer, emptying the receipts, debit cards, and scraps of paper from my wallet onto the floor around me, overwhelmed as I was with having finally arrived at the threshold toward which my entire life had been aimed. I was born to be there.

"How did you get here?"

"I walked."

"No, *what brought you here?*" I fished out the kachina, and with a spark I felt it unlock the doors as I placed it delicately in his hand.

"You gotta leave," he said.

Ha, I thought to myself. *I get it.* I picked up my wallet and its contents off the floor, like a lone performer stuffing his props back in his pockets at the end of a show with no audience. I remained optimistic; the jig would be up soon enough, the old double-fake was never lost on me. But the doors closed behind me and I didn't know what to think for the first time in months. Doubt had descended, so all would be lost.

"Watch it, asshole!" A drunk yelled my way as he sped up the business route.

★

False doors. The eighth, seventh, sixth, fifth, a fourth dimensioner even suggested that the people wanted me gone, now, here, where money fouled the cutthroat on another weekend in the seed factory of the arms garden. In the binary of an American mob world, the planes of buildings moved on a carousel, mirrors flashing onto expanses, pink, pink, pink and green, *think, think, think, what was I thinking?* Knee-deep in wet cement I advanced fiendishly as it hardened around my feet, crick in my second broken neck, to any third party, the walking dead, the ghost of Christmas future, an overdose.

I tripped down the stairs three at a time. Two juveniles held open the gates to the Blue Line. A vacuum took my hair. Cosmic strings to after-lives cascaded in the finest shades of gray, a lightning quivered into the depths on steel and red cedar. I don't know how I had become so weak, *so afraid.*

"Will this take me... will this take me..."

"Where are you going?"

"Back...back..."

Handing me their whiskey bottle, they suggested I call home, pointing out the pay phone behind me. My mind forced its way through the collect call routine, each number a pain in my hand as it dialed them without me.

"What do you mean everything's changed?"

"Everything Dad."

Minutes later, the graveyard pickup threw me in the back of the ambulance, and we raced up the on-ramp to the hospital.

Perched in the windowsill of the ward, I watched the sun rise over Lake Michigan. When it was light enough, I would find a plastic palette of watercolors. It was so beautiful out there, over the water, I would almost have died for a single swim toward the horizon. But there was simplicity about this pane of glass that I was learning to love. Something in the world was silenced by the way it kept me suspended there, way above it all.

The only other inmate awake still believed he was in the secret service, and was on his sixth cup of decaffeinated coffee, pacing around the lounge and talking my ear off about the 'special organizational services.' Alan and Diana had sex in the laundry room again, and we watched another nature video after lunch.

8

Ted's Dad

Kathy

The glass doors caught my suitcase as I stepped into a hollow lobby and got onto the elevator, surrounded by doctors in scrubs and baggy-eyed visitors with paper coffee cups in their hands. One by one they stepped off at their appointed floor—cardiology, pediatrics, oncology. On seven, signs to "Psychiatric" led me to a steel door with a tiny window webbed with fine metal strands.

"You have to leave your suitcase and purse and anything you've brought for Max here. We've got to check everything. No sharps," which I learned included belts, nail clippers, pens, even the half-filled bottle of juice I had tucked under my arm.

I found Max lying in his bed, legs drawn up to his chest.

"Matty," I whispered.

He sat up and smiled—looking at me with a haunted kind of relief. I wrapped my arms around him, thankful to have my hands on my kid, his frame angular and sharp. His eyes retreated into hollow orbs above edged cheekbones; his body slouched with exhaustion. Ugly torn blisters, red and bleeding, covered his heels and toes. He turned onto his belly and I kneaded his shoulders, ran the heel of my hand along each side of his spine. He was so quiet and I wondered where his mind drifted. I had no inkling of what he was experiencing—whether he was glad or scared, reliving his days on the streets of Chicago, or lost somewhere else entirely.

For the past year, I'd tried to believe his first episode was a mistake, a fleeting shift of brain chemistry, the planets out of alignment. But I still worried about whether the Depakote held a place beside his alarm clock. I knew the medicine took its toll—caused his hands to shake, eyelids to grow heavy, mind to blur—and that sticking to the regimen would be hard for him, as it is for most who have this illness.

When he disappeared a week ago during his spring break, I feared the worst, picturing him vanishing among the homeless or laying unidentified in a Chicago morgue. I called every friend who might know where he'd gone, but no one was able tell me anything except that he had driven to Chicago with another student.

Night after night Ron cooked dinner, concerned for my health as he watched me push carrots around my plate. He urged me to get out of the house, take a walk, have lunch with a friend, his objectivity part of his practical approach to life and now my only thread to reason. At my massage office, I tried to leave my problems at the door, but I kept my phone in my pocket on vibrate and left my clients lying on the massage table when it rattled against my hip. When I was home and Ron at work, I tried to write but mostly I looked at a blank computer screen and waited out the hours with the phone beside me.

The call finally came late at night. Max was being trans-ported by ambulance to Northwestern Hospital. He was be-ing admitted to the psychiatric unit, unharmed but psychotic. I knew this was just the beginning of another episode and that I had to pull myself together. I told myself he would get through it just as he had the last, that his dreams would not be buried under the rubble of manic-depression, that every page studied, paper written, canvas painted wouldn't seem like a lie.

★

Nolan, Max's dad had flown to Chicago from Virginia. We met for lunch, hugging in one of those formal ways that didn't require any real demonstration of affection. I wished we could connect, that together we could mourn the dam-age to our son, but our loss was different. He'd been so re-moved, had his own life and his family problems back in Virginia. His world wasn't centered on Max and Jessi the way mine was. For me it was immediate, and I was ready to fight for Max with gloves firmly tied. As always, our conversation turned into a series of criticisms and blame. He was sure that Max's treatment had been all wrong, the subtext being, "you're an incompetent parent."

We walked to the windy shore of Lake Michigan. Nolan stopped to light a cigarette, cupping his hand over the flame, and took a long drag. "I don't think Mom ever told you about her brother."

"No." I waited for the rest.

"She never talked about him. Back then in Georgia I don't think my grandparents knew how to get help. They just kept him home. Mom thinks it was schizophrenia or manic-depression."

I was angry he'd never mentioned his family history before. He must have known it was a significant part of Max's genetic history and vital information for his doctors. I couldn't understand his reluctance. I had long shared the indications of illness in my own family tree. My mother had suffered from severe depression and had been hospitalized after her fourth child. She'd been given electroshock treatment to jolt her back to her old self.

And I'd heard the story of her brother, the Chicago cop whose death was ruled suicide. My mother and aunt had insisted he was killed by the mob, unwilling to believe the other less palatable story of mental illness. So there seemed to be plenty of anomalies in Max's gene pool. It's hard to shake your finger at a strand of DNA, but untangling the predispositions to bipolar disorder was already proving to be obscured by taboo. The secrets of families burdened by mental illness complicated the already rough terrain of diagnosis and prognosis.

"I'm going to head to the airport," Nolan said, glancing at his watch. "I might catch the Duke game on the big screen at the bar before I get a plane home." I ground the cigarette he threw to the pavement into shreds, angry he was leaving Max, but at the same time relieved I wouldn't have to deal with the tension between us.

The next day in a lounge bathed in greens and pinks, I sat with the chief resident, a social worker, and a med student, who melted into the pastel background of Monets that graced the wall. It crossed my mind that a Dali or Magritte would have been more to the point.

"Max's blood tests show traces of cocaine and marijuana," the chief resident said as she flipped through her chart.

The cocaine took things to a new level. I wondered whether Max did hard drugs when he was tipping into an episode or whether he tipped into an episode because he'd taken drugs. It was a chicken and egg conundrum, but clearly Max was more likely to be doing drugs once he crossed the threshold into mania. At this point I knew he could be headed for a drug problem if he wasn't already there. I also knew that drug and alcohol abuse would turn what was already bad into a colossal problem. I'd read that drug use reduces the effectiveness of medication and leads to poorer adherence, that it means more relapse and hospitalization, and corresponds to a higher suicide rate and makes imprisonment all the more likely.

Sixty percent of those with bipolar disorder also suffer from substance abuse. So the assumption seemed to be that if Max didn't yet have a drug problem, he probably would. From that point, he was routinely included in substance abuse group therapy at Northwestern. He attended these sessions willingly, though he considered himself a rookie among the seasoned and disastrously addicted.

I spent hours in the psychiatric unit that week, interrupted only by walks along Lake Michigan or wanderings through the Water Tower, a vertical mall just blocks from my hotel. I often ended up in the bookstore, sitting on a stepstool with yet another book about bipolar disorder open in my lap. I studied the pages, eighty on medication alone: SSRI's, MAOI's, Benzodiazepines, anti-psychotics, calcium channel blockers, and drug complications.

Somewhere in these pages, I hoped I'd find answers from the experts. But their advice was thin. I needed something more immediate. So I began my own list:

#1—Try to smile when you walk onto the psych unit.
#2—Remember that normal is overrated.
#3—Don't give up the battle with the insurance company and their message machines.
#4—Control yourself when the doctor who says he's always in by seven doesn't show up until you decide to go get lunch and is gone by the time you get back.
#5—Never cry in front of Max.
#6—Call your sister and cry to her instead.
#7—Remember to eat and sleep.
#8—Pretend you're not afraid.
#9—Know that Max and I will get through this.
#10—When things seem hopeless, reread the sentence in the book that says, "Winston Churchill had manic depression."

★

When I arrived on the psych unit for visiting hours each day, Diana was usually hovering near the nurse's station, her unwound cornrows leaving her hair a wild, finger-in-the-socket fuzz.

"Hey, Max's mom. Follow me. I'll take you to the man." Diana knew everyone on the unit and most of their visitors. She wrapped her arm through mine and strutted down the hall, completely manic and having the time of her life.

"Bitch," she muttered at Gina as we passed her. Gina's glare was like a punch in the stomach. You could almost hear the whoosh as it took the breath right out of your lungs.

It was several days before I realized that Betsy, who was constantly straightening magazines, dusting, and throwing stuff in the trash, was not in fact on the staff. One of the nurses just gave me a "that's the way it is" shrug when Betsy picked up my full coffee cup and deposited it in the trash.

I sat with Max as he drew at a table where windows overlooked Lake Michigan. I watched a series of three beautiful pastels emerge—recording the water as the light changed and the clouds drifted across the sky. Charles sometimes came to sit with us, knowing that I probably had a pack of cinnamon gum in my pocket. His hand quivered as he unwrapped a stick and folded it between his teeth. His shaved head revealed tattoos that tendriled up the back of his neck and wound around his ears. He'd been in prison and was ostensibly here for drug addiction, but the rumor on the unit was that he was in the mob and hiding out in the ward. *Farfetched*, I thought, until I remembered where I was, how implausible life had become, and how real what happened here was.

On Thursday night, family and patients gathered in a room scattered with chairs. As people settled in, a social worker began with an invitation to share. A man named Ted took center stage. He was about thirty-five, blue-eyed, strikingly handsome, and charmingly bipolar. Ted's dad sat next to him. Ted was contrite and his dad was angry.

"I am not giving him any more money," his father said. "It's an endless cycle. He gets manic, spends everything he has, runs up his charge cards, and then comes to me. I'm just not doing it anymore."

I refused to believe that I could someday be Ted's dad, fed up, at wit's end, and ready to give up on my son. But obviously he hadn't given up either, as here he sat beside his son in a support group.

Over the next week, Max slowly improved, but he continued to be manic and at times delusional. It was clear to the doctors that Max would need more time, at least another week, maybe two. I knew my presence on the unit was only comforting me and that I should go home to regroup.

"I'll be back as soon as you're ready, Matty," I promised, leaving him supplied with gum, chips and candy bars before I hurried out the door.

It wasn't until years later that I realized Max had received the best care he would ever get at Northwestern. In hospitals like these, often teaching hospitals, treatment usually involves a holistic approach, involving a team of social workers, occupational therapists, and psychiatrists working with one another and directly with patients and families to collaborate on treatment plans and medication regimens. The staff is up to date on cutting edge, evidence-based medicine, and therapy involves one-on-one meetings with patients as well as group and families sessions. Restraints are seldom if ever used. Before release, an extensive outpatient plan is developed. At Northwestern Max never felt captive and keeping him in the hospital until he was completely stable was never a question.

★

I spoke with Max every day as he slowly got better. He looked forward to coming home and joked about the hospital food. He wanted to know what class Ron was teaching and how I was progressing on finding an agent for the mystery I'd just finished. Conspicuously absent was a conversation about what this episode meant to him or what he'd lost, which was more than just the chance to graduate this spring.

"What about the car?" he asked.

"It hasn't turned up. I think it's gone, Matty. It really

doesn't matter."

A week later, Max was waiting for me when I arrived, a smile lighting his face. Three weeks hospitalized, he was on the other side of the threshold with me, grateful, anxious, and free. When we stepped outside to the street, he lit a cigarette and took a deep drag as he got his bearings.

"Let's try to find my car."

I knew I was crazy to go along with this, but like Max, I too believe in finding ways to make things work out. Still I was unsure about what we'd do if we actually found the thing parked on the street in front of some stranger's house. I guessed we'd knock on the door. If it was the right one, a crack dealer would answer. He'd recognize Max, who would ask for the keys, which the dealer would gladly hand over because he remembered Max as the kid who loaned him his car for several weeks.

On the train, Max gazed out the window, watching for some familiar landmark. I had doubts that he could find his way back through the maze of his manic travels.

"This is it. Let's get off."

We retraced his path. He recognized a small park where the grass was now turning green and daffodils were popping though the earth. We stood in the middle of the park as Max studied the perimeter and pointed to a corner store where he'd bought cigarettes. We walked up one block and down the next in a neighborhood of peeling paint, broken blinds, and yards strewn with rusting bikes and old refrigerators. We passed garden statues of the Virgin Mary and planters filled with faded plastic flowers, scanning each block for the Smurf blue Honda among primer coated low-riders.

Max was sure we were close, but we finally had to give up the search for our flight home. I was relieved, but disappointed. His sketchbook, clothes, books, music, and his car were all gone. And we'd failed to restore a piece of his life as it was. A month later, Max watched his friends graduate without him.

9

This is Where

Max

It was a law, I was told, you can't sleep on a restaurant table. It was about 4:30 in the morning, and I was disquieted by my reflection in the window of the Greek café across the street from my apartment tangent to the Bowery. I frequently woke up suffocating in my closet apartment, my breath frozen in a deep, dry cough, over the rattle of a yellowing air conditioner spilling the ash of twenty-first-century New York in a swirl above my face. It was too hot to turn off the machine, but I doubt it would overcome the illusion anyway. It was summer in the City.

I thought islands were supposed to have palm trees. It's a wonder this place had any trees at all. I still saw it from the outside, but I could see myself seeing it. And it was like nothing I had seen before. There had to be a plan, we just couldn't make it out. But you know if you think about it too much you'll drown in it. Don't get me wrong, the whole thing was fascinating, truly the ninth wonder, or at least it would be once it was underwater. It would fill its potential, like any of God's ideas, or so I would have assumed.

Of course it was of no consolation to me at the time. It didn't look good for me either. I was halfway through my eight week New York Studio School painting atelier. I'd insisted on following through with it, despite my rocky spring and the concern of my parents, who anticipated this rather ruthless depression. Simple arithmetic. But I was a little bullheaded at the time, and for this I was nothing if not regretful by the month of July.

Looking through the café window as the city turned phthalo, I held back the vomit. Somebody else's nightmare, this place made me sick. When they at last awoke, New York would flow in rivers, and I would find a place in the knickerbocker sweep toward Greenwich Village, where I would once again buy a large coffee on 8th and Broadway before I got on the school bus we chartered to Long Island every day to work on our plein air paintings.

I'd put the coffee between my feet, lean my head against the window frame cracked to the island at rush hour, and wish we'd never get there, that the bus could just keep going and going forever, with my skull thumping against the window falling in and out of consciousness all the way to the Arctic. The jerking awake was part of the going back to sleep, my head nodding like I was unsure of my agreement about something.

Someone would shake me awake when we arrived, and I'd step out into the dew, delivered into a dream world to which I daily returned to solve the problems of the unconscious. To these concerns I understood art spoke, and at the time I didn't have a therapist so I took my chances. I'd slug down the cold coffee and get my easel from the shed like everyone else. I'd take it past the rectangular rows of shrubs and little stone boys spewing water into the morning sunlight, poised under the giant seashell at the top of a fountain, through the rose garden, the bent-up wheels of my push cart bouncing their way across the big meadow to the same Sycamore I had been painting for weeks. I might finally fall asleep again in the shade of its twisted trunk.

If I could be found, that week's visiting critic would wake me and suggest a different temperature for the sky. I was not what anyone would have called "a visionary," squinting hard at every stroke, sure it wasn't the one I intended. Simply a bad attitude under the circumstances, I should have been expressing my emotional terror, but I was a twitch in the all-seeing-eye, and God knows I didn't want another disappointing mess.

Still, I tried to put my all into the class, prompt for the noon critique at one, another at seven, then the break away for the sunset painting. Halfway in the dark, we were told to have faith in hoped for outcomes, a subject about which you might have guessed my opinion. Yet as the light disappeared completely, I reached out for the first time and stroked the accident on a pitch-black rectangle.

Two weeks prior, I had never used oil paint, and it was just another reason to off myself. And indeed it was hard to keep at bay the rattle of those little death promises even while painting landscapes at a manor that can only be compared to the set of *The Sound of Music*, on a thirty inch palette that would've broken Botticelli's heart. Though I had doubts about trucking all this shit through "the field," Sunnyside turpentine *smelled good*, twenty-two colors spread out in a double rainbow *looked good*, and my easel folded up to make a little wood suitcase. And look at those rolling hills, somewhere the sea, the groundskeeper by the pond, oak benches and parasols. A yellow dress, just over there, against the echoing green. There was something nauseating about how sweet it was, but I had to hand it to painting, it passed time.

Though suicidal ideation may have been buried for the afternoon, the shadow of the next fourteen hours would creep over my lap as soon as we departed back to the island. Spot lights waved over the criminals of Washington Square by sundown on Friday, placing me in the movie theatre on 2nd Ave, creeping to my seat shiftier than Lee Harvey Oswald. Looking over my shoulder from my position by the wall, I was sure I'd been fingered again. But fifty faces looked right through me as I bowed before them and exited politely as popcorn fell at Jurassic Park III.

It was just the movies for God's sake. A twenty-one year old from anywhere that used to like things such as friends and music, I should have been having the time of my life. I understood there was a lot to do in the greatest city on earth. But so it seemed, New York was dead at night. The locals would tell me I missed the whole thing, this place was just an amusement park now, you had to be so tall to ride, it closed at ten sharp. And so I frequented this Greek diner, where they could have cared less how long I sat there drinking burnt coffee and staring blankly at my disappointing sketches of the empty chairs and tables.

But the moon, I noticed, had been rising earlier. When I looked over the edge of the roof of my apartment, I could see the space between the buildings. Clearly nine floors was enough to do the job, but it no longer seemed like I would just disappear into the black.

★

"This is where...This is who...This is how..." said my father, as we took in the spectacle from the window of the barbecue dump he decided on for lunch. I picked at a piece of dry cornbread while he dropped down a half-rack of swine. For a Georgian he seemed to know everything about the Bowery, but everything I heard went into the same void, just making it bigger. He was a little concerned but he still managed to enjoy his weekend up north by keeping us on the go and the conversation light.

But the two of us couldn't have made a worse duo on Wall Street; I had an aversion to establishment and especially disestablishment, so forget Central Park. According to my internal catalogue of end game logistics, it wasn't so glamorous to jump off the East tower anymore. What my father had to realize was that I could have played "tell me something worth living for" all day. A game rigged in my favor, he decided the museum was the next destination and set a course on the subway map. It was the weekend so the scene was set; a mob of people moved through the annals of the Great Museum like worms through the spice.

My father contemplated the landmarks of the impressionist wing. Quickly falling for Monet, he reached out and brushed his finger against the purple ridges of a water lily. I could only rudely suggest he not touch the national treasures, using that same hoarse whisper he once used with my half-sisters when in public, though privately I felt for his artlessness. In his 58 years of life, this was the first time he had ever set foot in an art museum. He was from the south, and I was from the old west. The citizens of Colorado Springs seemed to agree that art and the military didn't mix and they might have been right; it was no secret what really drove the economy in those parts so it was never really a question. I still couldn't stop asking myself how they attracted all this art into one little space, the great majority of it in underground vaults, but I guess the rest of the country has to live in darkness for the sake of posterity.

Down the hall, Annette Giacometti was still all miked up, like she just put her finger in the socket for the tenth time just to stay awake on day fifty while Al gave her another whipping on the stretched fabric, putting off another child with a curse, crossing her boxing gloves over her sex like she was the last woman on earth. It was a love triangle made to be broken in a gray room, where it finally realized its potential *to move*, through the dark ecstasy of the human catastrophe, decadence to the art connoisseur.

Picasso's *Woman Ironing* took another blow with her rigid arms, when I was finally alone with her at the Guggenheim, squared off like she was *made* to be bent over a table. That line down her back brought me to tears every time, like a true masochist I returned for another round. Off goes the alarm again. Kicked out, half-dead 5th Avenue feels walkable all the way downtown.

10

Corrective Shoes

Kathy

It was 7:30 in the morning and already hot. I found Max on the roof of his apartment building, sitting on the wall, staring at the space between his feet, cigarette dangling between his fingers, coffee cup beside him. The East Village rooftops surrounded us—flat and black. It was June and Max was in New York for an eight-week intensive course in painting at the New York Studio School where he enrolled before his manic episode last spring. I was there to provide moral support and, of course, to reassure myself.

His depression seemed different this time—more angst ridden, self-critical and unsure. He hadn't slept more than a few hours in several days. I hated it when he went up to the roof. I told myself that he would never simply let himself fall. On that Sunday morning we perched up there together as the Village came alive below. Soon we would join the masses, making our way through the confusion to the subway on our way to the Metropolitan Museum of Art. Max studied every piece, getting close. I had never spent much time thinking about the world of art until my son's passion grew. Now I wanted him to explain the pieces and evaluate them, tell me about the artist. But at the time Max had a "see what you see and like what you like" attitude.

While he was at school, I roamed aimlessly through the Village and Soho. The tattered homeless panhandled as people nearby sipped lattes; pinstripes hurried past pierced eyebrows and pink hair; moms with strollers waited at bus stops beside old women in stained polyester and white corrective shoes. Narrow brick buildings lined one street after the next, habitations for restaurants, dress shops, bars, and tattoo parlors. Max's apartment was among them, where across the street, the Orthodox Ukrainian Church competed with the Sing Sing Karaoke Bar.

Up seven flights and breathless, I fumbled with the keys and stepped into the narrow hallway of torn linoleum and scarred mustard walls. The entire apartment must have once been a one bedroom, now divided into three with a kitchen and a single bathroom—a master feat of exploiting limited space in order to charge $733 a month for each of the three cubicles, and this, they said, was extremely cheap. Strangers resided in the other two bedrooms, their doors always closed.

I would settle at the tiny desk in Max's room and turn to the last page in my notebook where I'd scrawled a list of medicines. Some were crossed out, new ones taking their place. The current list included:

40mg   Geodon 2x a day
400mg Lamictal at night
150mg Wellbutrin 2x a day
900mg Lithium at night

Every time I called his psychiatrist, it meant an adjustment. Not sleeping--more Geodon. Still not sleeping, less Geodon. Max sinking deeper into depression, more Lamictal, more Wellbutrin. Each time the doctor changed something, he told us we would have to wait. So we waited. Another adjustment and I wondered what was working and what wasn't, but today's solution would be simple, an over the counter sleep aid from the corner drug store.

Max came home late, exhausted and overwhelmed. He didn't know whether he was up to the intensity of the class. Attending the New York Studio School was an opportunity for Max to study with well-regarded artists, but just a month out of the hospital, he was sleepless and depressed and his self-confidence was shot. He needed to make a decision about whether he should stay or return home with me, where he could recuperate, see his doctor every week, and be in a supportive environment. Part of me wanted him to come home, but I worried about what giving up would mean for him.

The next morning, he was still undecided —stay or leave, stay or leave. Finally, he put a shaky hand on the ladder, pulled himself into his loft and got back in bed.

"Shit, I guess I'll just go," he said minutes later, throwing the covers to the floor. He jammed his stuff into his backpack and walked out. I was surprised by the relief that washed over me.

A few days later, I watched him head up 7th Street to class as my cab passed on the way to the airport. Dressed in a tweed newsboy hat and worn jeans, he smoked and walked, eyes on the sidewalk. God knows what he was thinking.

11

Black Flower

Max

"Heeey Max, how's it goin'? Yeahhh greeeaat, listen Max there's been some concern around campus and I'm sure everything is fine, but just to, I don't know, *satisfy those concerns*, I thought you might join me to see Missus Tischler, the social services coordinator, for a quick chat and check-in." I shouldn't have been surprised that I was talking to Grinnell's dean of student affairs at the front door of my apartment on my day off.

"I want you to know that I share these concerns with everyone and have been considering the best course of action with my friend Pat here." We had been discussing my differences with the traditional structure of class.

Just the previous Monday, for instance, it all seemed like a comedy of errors in my poetry class. Dr. Frick, where was Dr. Frick? Late again. Just time to unbuckle my dad's gold watch with the quartz face I'd smashed, an event that placed its little gold fingers at my disposal. And so I bent the second hand skyward. I congratulated myself. On the sill by the giant wood compass, it looked exceptional, a motioning glimmer of light beneath my masterpiece in dry-erase markers executed with the fury of Michelangelo berserk on twenty angels.

The tip of the gold wire cut its tiny circle in the air as Dr. Frick paced before my giant rainbow mural accented with its 24 Karat machine, flushed as he dipped back and forth across my diachronic charts and ad hoc family trees, fumbling for an excuse for his poetic tardiness. But it just came out all wrong, adding to the distracted and uneasy posture of my classmates, scene framed by my nest of sunshine yellow canaries and my chrome green Mark XIX.

"You know I've about had it with this, Max. When is it gonna stop? What did I do to deserve this? Is this how you act in every class? You're holding us all back, and for what?" and so on and so forth. Tired of literary criticism I buried my head in my arms and tried to sleep through his lecture.

"Max must already know this." Everyone laughed, even me, revealing my bluff; I hadn't slept in days.

"Maybe I need a little time off," had been one of my favorite sayings of late.

"Wellllll, Max," repeated the dean, maybe you wouldn't mind then, just coming with me for a half-hour, a half-hour at most, just to check in, and then we can address these concerns surrounding school, talk about a plan that suits you."

Pat agreed to walk me to the clinic, sharing with me a little fresh air for what promised to be a long stay indoors. As the dean crept half a block back in her LeSabre, we walked together, for now the best of friends, on either side of an invisible fence, Pat with his fingers just touching my elbow in a way, making sure I'd be okay, that I'd make it to my little physical but not exactly sure that I was that bad off.

"From the looks of it, I'm really gonna have to do this," I said. Pat lit up and laughed through his nose.

"That's the look of it. What a bitch."

The air warm and heavy, the light like purple strings stretched to their limit, the clouds winding up the horizon and putting sunshine to sleep up the center of Sixth. A ketamine evening, like diamonds in cocoa powder the whole town was as if evacuated.

"All of the above," I said a fifth time. Of course there was no such answer, but the diagnostic Q&A very clearly produced the suspected symptoms, drawing one last laugh from Pat. Ear right next to The Mouth, I cried out with the sting of The Voice, as my friend was escorted from the room. Our coordinator did her job pointedly, as did the ambulance driver, who rushed me to the institution.

★

My mind raced as a strong arm took my legs at the ankles, another dug his knees in my back, one cleared his throat and another should have grunted, as a third yanked down my pants and penetrated my anus with what I could only hope was his large index finger. *I know you're there, this isn't funny anymore, avant-garde, revolutionary guard, whoever the fuck is still on guard, mayday, mayday. It's that fucking Dean. She set this up, that goddamn dirty official, that fucking whore.*

"Awww... Ahhh... No, seriously, thank you for that," I said as he felt for my prostate, as though he meant to turn me on, and then off, and then on again with the switch of my entrails. They dropped a generous dose of Thorazine in my right ass cheek and left the door open on their way out.

"Wow what a welcome party! Thanks a lot you NURSE HOOKERS!"

Not exactly paranoid, I was nothing if not concerned. They'd have no problem getting rid of another body in these parts, known only for their corn and swine. This is the plate of America for God's sake, limb from limb, that's how she does it. They'd just toss me in one of the many cesspools of farm run-off and pesticide corrupt fish, or so I mused, even the chickens stayed away from 'the pond' in Iowa. Or I'd be pig food or show up in your dog's bowl, hell if they wouldn't just burn me alive. Not a soul would smell it over all the hog shit and it ain't no stroke of genius to baffle the Cedar Rapids Sheriff I was sure.

Dreary on the needle, still unwieldy were my conspiracy theories as I leaned my way down the hall, burning my shoulder on the wall to a door slightly ajar, behind which I warily slipped.

"I have called you, my disciples, to be here together at once," a voice proclaimed from the bed.

Cross-legged, bearded, and overweight, a mélange of Siddhartha and an ancient Gaul, Tom was silhouetted by an electric sky locked in the last signs of dusk.

★

The staff broke out the hallway cots; it was that time of year again. I don't know what it is about the spring. Some say it's the star spectrum, the angle of the sunburst, Thanatos smacking his lips over another rebirth, the Ace of Cups or all the girls in shorts. But it's as though God wanted us to get it on together. On the flowers, on the trees, the asylum played its part beautifully in an ecosystem lacking for nothing.

Yes it was *foliex à plusieurs*, the madness of many, the groundhog had seen his shadow and we bipolars had that place staked out and not a day too soon. The beginning of the season at Pfizer, four o'clock on the mental highway's rush hour, millions were moved, billions were made, just as Tom predicted, the numbers were there. A line went up the screen, the transition had just that one seam, it was a take-over.

We crammed into the little smoking lounge, Marlboro 100s between our fingers and Newports tucked behind our ears, chain-smoking until we couldn't see each other in a comedy fit for kings. We roasted the world. The first in line ignited from an electric coil embedded in the wall and we monkey-fucked the rest. We all took note when someone new came in late, wove their way around our embers and lit off the coil. They became the butt of our inside joke.

It spread through the entire hospital. I laughed till I cried, hovered around the tube with my comrades. I needn't mention the radio, the substitute weather woman, tectonics and barely perceptible tremors. At dinner over plates of crud and punch our crowing revealed how ready we were to fight. Rowdy in the halls of the house of cards for *How to Host a Murder*, I recall the feeling, I could have never left it behind even if I had tried.

To tell you the truth I almost didn't care what it all really meant. All I knew was that Tom knew, and I guess that was good enough for me. Because you know I felt it. The map of time, shifting over the beaten green of an old coin-op pool table, my ass half-open through my paper dress, was pushed around by a piece of antler on an old stick of pine. My childhood pastime it couldn't have been more perfect.

At the break of course I put everything I had into the

follow through, making a snap that got a jump out of the nurses even behind their inch thick Plexi. Sometimes switching sides or pulling straws, Tom would take the odds, raising my hand when he picked up his cut. Some would say I was a natural, as went free the light when my neck was unkinked and I rose for another stroke, the gift of that prehistoric ecstasy all over a game of pool. I'm telling you it was magic. If it wasn't the work of God it was the perfected craft of the devil, and of course it didn't matter because all we could do was play.

★

I don't know if we underestimated them, or overestimated ourselves, but my socks cleaved to yellow specks of polonium-210 and I was starting to feel it. My jeans smelled like acid and there was jizz all over the hamburgers. They kept pushing that purple stuff off those clipboards, pens, and diamond rings, vigilante goon squads and Neo-Nazi doctors, solving us like they did the Jewish problem. I wasn't sure if I was the next Trotsky or just another Judas, the bag lady threw out my lithograph, they had us turning on each other.

Tom wasn't having it though. "Calm down. It's okay," he told me. But what he didn't understand was that these bugs would stop at nothing. They were pouring out of the walls and marching inside our mirrors with sweet corn straight from the steel closet. This whole thing was a set up and he was just going to sit there and take it, the shifting image flashing in his big glasses, a duet framed in translucent sepia fluttering over a reversible trance. Hair slicked over his skull, pretending to watch *Night Court*, he disregarded me.

Oh, Tom, break me out, send me on the silver through the cracks of the dying Columbines. Violet, red. Do you remember that yellow? You do. I know you do. We had only wet our feet as darts fled through the forest to meet us. They had done this before, and of course so had you. The story went on for me, but I was barely there to bear its witness: more vague flashes of what happened in a trance, the voice of many waters and its little submarine, the grain elevator and the big red barn. The farmer still woke at dawn, and the sow wallowed in the mire as the bull turned to his own vomit again.

Quick was the antibiotic, sloppy was the job, corralled, we forged bonds. On hooks in the slaughterhouse we swayed, nobody was ever so intimate as we. Hanging inverted together on the precipice of death, around our abdomens they drew uncareful lines. It was not a surgical incision at last, it was an old fashioned hiding. We were unhooked and put back in the rodeo. There we fell over each other as upon us the eye fell again.

Escorted from the ring one by one, we were all fit under the sheets at once, breathing slowly as we were told again that it was just a dream. In a flash spring had passed, and the curtains privately unfolded over the true secret as the lights went down. There we descended to meet our flattened utopias, in the court where psychosis blooms its black flower, unleashing its flock of insects. And so I cried as I let my arm fall from beneath the fabric to feel the hand of another human being, dying to believe someone was still on the other side.

12

Cedar Rapids

Kathy

My heart broke for Max, and then I was angry with him. I felt overwhelmed. Still recovering from the last episode, I wondered if I could get through another. Then I felt like a self-involved child when it was Max who truly suffered. Then I was swimming in anger again. This was the end of the semester and I feared it would be his last opportunity to graduate.

I left before the sun came up and arrived in Cedar Rapids as it was going down. Max was in his room sitting on the bed, hands gripping the mattress. He smiled when he saw me. We sat together, arms around each other. He was thin, pale, his hands trembled.

"Matty, are you okay?" I asked, knowing how stupid the question was.

He responded in quick one-line rhymes and non sequiturs that I couldn't follow. Finally he told me three male nurses had held him down, stripped off his clothes, and done a cavity search at intake. I couldn't believe what I was hearing.

"What happened with my son yesterday?"

"Max was uncooperative," the male nurse sitting behind the counter said, knowing exactly which son was mine and to what I was referring.

"What do you mean, he's sick. He has no idea what's happening to him. All he needs is a little time and space."

"We gave him plenty of both. It took 45 minutes to get him to change into a hospital gown."

"He told me he was restrained and that you did a cavity search."

"We took a team approach to get him admitted and we don't do cavity searches," he said.

It was his word against Max's. I realized how naïve my expectations about treatment in psychiatric wards had been. As the days passed, I could see that a culture of mistreatment, incompetence, and indifference was entrenched on the unit.

Unfortunately, this is often the best there is to offer in a system in which funding cuts have prevented any semblance of comprehensive services. Those services were supposed to become available in the 60s when most asylums were closed because of the effectiveness of new psychotropics, the horrible conditions in these facilities, and the shifts in funding under Medicare and Medicaid. Hundreds of thousands of the mentally ill were released.

The caveat—a coordinated community mental health care system nationwide was to be developed in their place. That never happened because there was no funding ever set aside for that purpose. In 2003 the New Freedom Commission on Mental Health declared the mental health care "a system in shambles." Still nothing has changed but the further deterioration of the system and the people who need it.

Writes Michael Fitzpatrick, the Executive Director of the National Alliance on Mental Illness "many years of bad policy decisions have left emergency rooms, the criminal justice system, and families to shoulder the burden of responding to people in crisis." The mental health care system is underfunded, uncoordinated—the term "system" a misnomer. There's a shortage of beds for the severely ill and more resources are being eliminated every day. Few adequate crisis programs exist and there is no mechanism to respond to those with symptoms who don't recognize they need treatment. Those who do find treatment can find the "cure" worse than the illness itself.

It's no wonder that Max resists hospitalization at all costs. And now I was the one who wanted him out, when all I'd wanted two days ago was to get him hospitalized. This place was just a holding tank. I'd spoken with the doctor only once, a five minute conversation in the hallway in which he told me how difficult Max had been, instigating trouble on the unit. The doctor was anxious to release him and in the process ridding himself of me, another troublesome presence. After two days, he informed me that Max would be released the next morning.

But when I returned for him that morning, they weren't letting him go anywhere. There had been trouble the night before. I found Max in his room, anxious and confused. I tried to distract him with checkers, cards, the TV, but he couldn't sit in one place for ten seconds. He wandered into the poolroom, the cafeteria, back to his own room. Not knowing how to help him, I sat on the couch and waited for his periodic returns.

Two middle-aged patients joined me on the sofa, one on

either side. "Max was locked in his room last night," one reported without introduction.

"Do you know why?"

"Not really. There was a lot of commotion though."

Before I could find out more, Max returned to tell me I had to leave. "Something's happening. It's bad. You have to go now, Mom." I saw nothing unusual as I glanced around at the relative peace in the unit. "How about I sit with you while you eat dinner?"

"No Mom, you've got to get out of here. Now."

He was extremely paranoid, and my presence was just making it worse. I gave him a hug and fled through the door before I fell apart. I barely made it back to my hotel. I sat on the side of the bed, head in hands, staring blankly at the stains on the carpet.

★

"Max was blessing people," said the unit supervisor. I thought blessing people seemed pretty innocuous.

"He was standing on a chair, obscuring the cameras. He took a magic marker to the walls in the smoking room."

"Did you try to talk to him?"

"He wasn't directable."

"And you locked him in his room?"

"We don't lock people in."

I didn't know what to think. I had never known Max to be threatening or hostile, sick or not. I wondered what she meant by "directable," and whether they had tried simple reason or just presumed that was never an option.

When I got to the hospital the next day, Max was sitting on the floor near the door, curled in on himself, arms wrapped around his legs, head on his knees.

"I thought you were dead."

"I'm fine, Matty. Everything is okay."

I stayed the entire day. I followed him to the poolroom, where he was edgy as he racked up the balls and began a game with another patient. Suddenly, he pushed all the balls in the pockets, grabbed both pool cues and slammed them on the table. He stormed over to his opponent, shook his fist at him, and pointed his finger at the tip of the guy's nose. I was stunned by his anger and feared the response it might stir in a place like this. But Max just stomped out. I found him in the lounge, gazing at the TV, feet perched on the coffee table, unable to explain himself.

As I walked to the nurse's station to get Max apple juice, a social worker stopped me in the hall.

"The insurance company wants to know why Max isn't home in Colorado instead of here in Iowa."

"He was here when he got sick. This is where he goes to school," I explained, confused about why she was asking. After all, she had to know he was a student and had been admitted with the school's assistance.

"Why is he still going to school in Iowa?" she asked.

"Because Grinnell is the school he's chosen, and Grinnell is in Iowa. It's where he wants to study," I said, completely amazed that she was asking.

"Well, the insurance company wants an explanation."

They didn't want to pay for his care "out of system." In other words, they wanted to dictate where Max lived and studied.

"That's just the way it is," I told her through clenched teeth and left her standing in the hallway with her clipboard.

Early the next morning, I returned to the hospital because the doctor had informed me that he was again ready to release Max. We both knew he wasn't even close to being stable. I could only guess that the insurance company was pressuring the hospital. In any case Max had gotten worse in the time he'd been there and I just wanted him out.

The discharge nurse gave me the standard brown paper bag—Ativan, 1 mg, every 4 hours, with an extra .5 mg as needed; Zyprexa, 5 mg at 8:00 and 6:00 and every six hours as needed; Geodon, 20 mg at bedtime; Lithium 600 mg at 8:00 am, 900 mg at 6:00 pm. The Lithium was in liquid form and the eyedropper didn't even fit in the bottle.

I kept the car doors locked while we drove. Max lit one cigarette after the other, sometimes two or three burned in the ashtray. At rest stops I rushed to get out of the bathroom before him. I tried to pour the Lithium into the eyedropper to measure the correct dosage and it dripped candy red all over Max's shirt. At every gas station, he wanted to buy another pack of cigarettes.

"You've already got three packs in the car," I told him.

He bought energy drinks and coffee, feeding the mania the drugs were supposed to be smothering.

"How are you doing, Matty?" I asked.

"Don't worry, Mom," he comforted as he put his arm around my shoulder or held my hand.

He'd slide in one of his tapes and turn the volume up, then switch to the radio, then put on a Joseph Campbell *Power of Myth* tape, then go back to his mix tape, light a cigarette, take two drags, and throw it out the window. Light another and put Campbell back on. He tried to sleep without success. Round and round he went through the slate Midwest plains.

Hundreds of geese flew in formation over fields of harvested corn. A hawk sat on a fence pole at the side of the highway. Max wasn't interested.

"Lots of grays and browns now, but soon it will be spring."

"I don't think I'll see another spring."

"Of course you will, Matty." My voice fractured. "Spring is only a few weeks away. The flowers will be blooming and the trees will be turning green."

"Maybe."

We kept going, out of Iowa, through Nebraska, and finally into Colorado. As the meds wore off, he got anxious, and talked about "they." He wasn't able to tell me who "they" were, but I gathered "they" listened in on our conversations, were subversive and bad. Very bad. I tried to keep his attention on the snowstorm that was building outside our windows, hoping he could rest his mind in the hypnotic swirls of snowflakes long enough to get him home.

I tried to figure out what his next dose was supposed to be. The storm had turned into a blizzard, and I began to imagine the worst—stranded on the side of the road in deep drifts with Max lost in a world of delusions. I kept my eyes glued to the road and handed him the bag. He took the Ativan, then retrieved what I was sure was the same bottle and spilled out another.

I kept going, creeping along at 25 mph. Snow blew across the windshield and piled up on the road. Finally, we pulled off the main highway and onto the gravel road that led to our driveway. My husband was waiting.

The next morning at 5:00, the sky was still just a dusty glow in the east when I suddenly awoke, panicked as I realized that the lights were on in the living room. By the time I got to the kitchen, Max and Ron were walking in from the garage. Ron had heard the door open and found Max in the car, keys in the ignition, and on his way to take his clothes to

Goodwill. I poured him a glass of milk and handed him an Ativan and a Zyprexa. He went downstairs, took a shower and shaved off his beard. He was completely dissociated, but ten minutes later he somehow agreed to admit himself voluntarily to the psychiatric hospital in Colorado Springs.

★

Every day, we looked for some sign that he was getting better—a smile, a softening around his eyes, a request for a Twinkie, anything. I couldn't help but believe his current condition was the result of the treatment in Cedar Rapids. I suppose it was not so simple. With every episode, Max's condition was bound to get worse, the illness harder to treat, his behavior more extreme.

But inferior treatment made everything worse. After nine days in the hospital, nothing had changed. The doctor adjusted medications and the drugs kept piling up.

"There is risk that Max will develop permanent psychosis," the doctor told us. "He hasn't responded at all to any of the medicine."

Ron and I drove home in silence. What more was there to say? There was no planning for the future. I couldn't fight the fear that I might never again be able to connect with Max. That we'd never be able to talk about his art, his goals, his joys and sorrows, or his latest girlfriend. That he could be lost in his own world forever.

Days went by and Max remained edgy, verging on panic at times, fatalistic and delusional. We often found him pacing the halls or fluttering among the other patients, never settling in one place unless he'd just been given a strong dose of Ativan. Then we'd find him lying on his bed, face buried in his pillow, knees drawn to his chest. He said he would never get out. If we stayed too long, he got anxious and agitated and sometimes he didn't want us there at all.

One night, he called at 2:00 a.m., worried we would never return. "Of course, we'll be there, Matty. I will never, ever leave you."

Finally, Max found his way out of the void. It was the first day of spring. When Ron and I arrived for visiting hours, we found him sitting in a chair with his feet up on a table, sketching the face of the woman nearby. Immediately, I could see the transformation—in his posture, in the way his pencil moved around the sketch pad, in the smile on his face when he saw us. I was astonished how abruptly he'd recovered. I don't think even the doctor knew why.

On a May Day two months later, I found myself sitting beside Jessi and Ron at Grinnell College watching the graduates file in and take their seats. Max was among them.

13

Candy Junkie

Max

I pulled my camera strap over my neck and put my right foot out into the untouched crystal bed. Letting my weight down I was suddenly waist deep in a snowdrift. My light meter was shot, but I let out a solitary laugh through the valley below my parent's new mountain home. It was all too perfect, the sky, a rich warm blue above.

I had a typically restless night. Twice a week I worked the graveyard shift at the Ute Pass Senior Residence, where I got an occasional wink on the couch while the eight elderly people in my care slept away eleven hours of a winter night. I watched Perry Mason or the documentary on the Musée d'Orsay through the long hours, occasionally swallowing a Percocet loose in the bottom of the medicine cabinet. Around 6:15 in the morning, I prepared a breakfast of oatmeal, toast, and scrambled eggs, or whatever was on the schedule for Wednesday.

I changed George's dirty diaper and tried to encourage him that it would be a great day today. I hefted up all 175 pounds of the 99 year-old Marion, who had probably been sitting in a pool of urine for twenty minutes while I pulled George's flannel shirt over his head and combed his hair to the side, his eyes always focused on the same spot on my upper left arm. When I yanked her pants off, Marion sometimes surprised me with a slap to the face, screaming bloody murder as if it were date rape at senior prom.

The rest of them could get up by themselves. Breakfast always came five minutes late on my shift, something noticed by all and inevitably commented on by Hampton and Ernie, who had been awake since five a.m. in their separate rooms, watching the sun creep into the woods and light up the red rocks. No doubt these early-risers were perfecting their complaints, which I could only overcome with the charm for which I was hired (I had, after all, no related experience whatsoever).

I reminded most of them of their grandson, if I weren't in fact mistaken for him. But what can I say? I liked old people and these folks were my friends. A plate of food in front of each of them, with all special modifications made, I poured the orange juice and gathered the little foggy-plastic cups of capsules, tablets, and liquids. Pinching them off an old cafeteria tray covered in a fresh piece of white paper, I set the respective medicines out in front of each of them.

I would walk home after my shift, stepping through holes in barbed wire fences, running from the local dogs as I made fresh tracks westerly. I'd say good morning to Mom while coffee brewed, anticipating the peace of taking photos on a winter Wednesday like a true aristocrat.

But it seemed my hobby had been perhaps forever hindered. I climbed the hill, stuck the broken camera in the closet, and examined the morphine pouch I swiped from the medicine cabinet at work. I'd fed Barbara her last meal a week ago, half a peanut butter and jelly sandwich and a molasses cookie. She had left behind her array of heavy pain medication: Roxicet for maintenance; Oxycontin for the light days; for the more trying nights, jumbo bags of Fentanyl, to which I was not yet disposed but guessed I would find quite fitting.

She died a relatively unconscious death moments after I left my last day shift, so she wouldn't be in need anymore, sadly but obviously. I meant no disrespect, but I was content that she was happy to be dead after a long struggle with bone cancer in the home. Despite the "Don't Resuscitate" order, she died with a breathing tube down her throat choking on her own blood. It just didn't seem right, and here I was the beneficiary.

But what can I say, I was a little bored up there in the mountains without a car. Having no penchant for needles, which I understood was the preferred street method, I read the directions, went into the bathroom, and slapped her patch of syrup on my shoulder. An hour later I was throwing up in the downstairs bathroom, still somehow chuckling to myself about my day thus far.

It was the beginning of 2002; the exhilaration had taken me. For the first time since I was five years old, I didn't have to go back to school that spring.

★

After a lazy game of pool, my best friend Louis and I bounced around in his old bronze Civic, known to us as the "Wakovan," bumping his latest find, tape deck wired to MP3, pulling on a oney packed with Purple Kush. Masta Ace's *Dis-*

posable Arts had just come out, but it could have been anything. I'm telling you we were hip hop heads to the end, a fact made clear as we crept up Ute Pass bobbing our heads with our elbows bent over the door frames. The west side of the Peak was aglow, as surreal as any hallucination floating in the sky behind the grazing horses in the mountain meadows and aspen groves spotting either side of the gravel roads of Covenanted Woodland West. We veered up the hidden driveway to my parents' wooden home.

Of course if this was my place, I would've outfitted it with some real speakers and a hot tub. But Ron's extremist Anglo-Saxon practicality and my mother's allegiance to the facts were attitudes garnered in the fifties; they were of course rock hard. So Mom paced, hovering like Inspector Clouseau hot on the trail of the pink cat, waving her looking glass over our dirty poems as if she would ever get a clue. But it was all mumbo jumbo to her, and like Method Man and Raekown we just kept feeding each other. Soon enough Louis trashed my mom in a heroic couplet. I couldn't top him and got fed up.

I assured Mom I was taking my medicine and kissed her cheek. I never expected her to buy it, but we had to have the act, and of course Louis just kept nodding his head. In any case she was dealing with a shared reality that was, above all, supposed to be occupied solely by me, so we ditched that pop stand like dogs off a leash.

We rolled back down Highway 24 to catch the last moments of the dusk from the mesa at the trailhead of Waldo Canyon, overlooking the winding highway and the broad mountain valley. The sun had fallen behind the mountains and the sky glowed cobalt, Venus ruthless in the west, the stars rose twinkling on this crystal clear night, and the moon lit up the whole canyon ice-cold.

As they say, there are friends with whom you can share anything. Manic depression in degrees runs through Louis's family, though I wouldn't have pointed to a diagnostic thread as the source of our agreement that a synchronicity so rounded should be taken in silence, as if we both recognize the delicacy of our placement, like a single utterance would shake free the constant shadow from its station or the granite beneath our feet. The highway below had been emptied of its cars, like roadblocks had been set in either direction, darkening the black serpent carving the mountainside.

I anticipated our descent, knowing there would be no turning back this time. There was nowhere to go, nothing to do. I would never eat another bite of food or read another word. I would never be able to look at my family again. They could only insist that nothing ever happened, that the stream flowed as it ever had, and I should rejoin it; that there are people who can help.

★

"What do you want me to do with that?" I asked, rhetorically, of my new Indian friends, looking down on the bed in 108 at two double fist-sized brown rolls of hash and two tall glass cigar vials a quarter full with ground up peyote. I took everything in front of me and stuffed it in my cargo pants and promised to return with the money.

"I don't know, you'll just have to trust me, I haven't got a dime," I insisted.

That much was true, but I had just started my morning and had that familiar sense of great things all around me. For me and others like me, such emotional states of extreme well-being are associated most closely with illness, and this, I suppose, they will call a paradox. And it's worthy of note that I hadn't slept more than a wink or two the past few nights, and everybody knows how much we all need slumber, and for a certain number of hours, 6-8 is what I hear. In the same breath they will say "we are all different" and we should accept each other as we are, but they mean to make an exception for the habits of the insane, by which they mean anybody who is plain too different.

But my two Indian companions only amplified my feeling of importance that day; tall lanky Daryl with his long silky black hair, his wife Dee, a pilgrim's nightmare, four and a half feet of witchcraft with wicked black eyes. A pair of hustlers with nothing much to lose but each other, that day partners in the bustling counterfeit drug market, involving me, a total stranger, in the matter when we'd met downtown twenty minutes prior.

However, the plentiful samples of "hash" and "peyote" were to no effect whatsoever, corroborated by my friend Travis who tried excessive amounts just to make sure. He traded a big chunk of brown gum for a handful of shrooms. We choked them down with a pitcher of Stroh's.

"I guess it's all subjective anyway," said Travis, who liked my story about the Indians.

Well, I hustled the corner anyway, easily uncovering a consumer base for the counterfeiters. Odorless and benign, I found the look of the thing was really paramount to its placebo effect. By appearance it was all virtually identical so I got no complaints. Later, I fished out some crumpled cash from the various pockets and dropped it on the pink and turquoise bedspread of 108.

"That's all you got?" asked Daryl, clearly happy to see

they could pay for a few more nights at the motel. Dee gave me a new belt and twenty bucks and we agreed to meet later.

★

I caught up with my friend Meg, whose toes were broken from ballet practice again. We limped together a few blocks to her friend's place to lay low for a while.

"Are you sure you should be breaking your toes though?"

"It's just part of it, Max."

I'd just sold a handful of whathaveyou, so I wouldn't be able to stay long. But a little buzzed on psilocybin, I felt good, *great* even, like this was what I was supposed to be doing in the threshold of an open door with my generation, like there was nothing else but this fine fuchsia electricity in the walls and the mind's adventure in a bedroom with strangers over a cassette of Bitch's Brew.

But rising up was the feeling these moments of social harmony were but corpuscles of time-off, decoys set into the waters of more important things. The longer the sun was down, the more I couldn't resist the feeling. I grabbed the big ring of keys from the hallway table, somewhere on which was the key for the tricked-up Acura parked out front.

I unlocked the door, rolled down all the windows, and adjusted the mirrors as I put 'er in gear.

"Now I can get all this stuff done," I thought as I pulled out onto Nevada Avenue, flying up and down its dips at seventy or so, white knuckled, eyes fixed on the road, chuckling while punching it, butterflies fluttering in my stomach. "I'll just throw the shipment in the back," I said through my teeth as I pictured loading up the trunk with the most magnificent intoxicants not yet desired by the white man, racing around town ducking the po with my superior horses. Reckless in a lucid dream I was just enjoying the top of the world. Enough reason to put aside any discomfort about the immediate situation, in terms of stealing a car while tripping and making a big scene of it, tires screaming like a newborn dragon as I punched it back south, whipping my tail end around the six lane intersection as though I had always known how to drive like a fire-breathing maniac.

"That's it! I'll just hand over the keys to a single buyer and be on with my night," I murmured to myself as I raced past my childhood home at 1712.

"Damn it if this isn't some kind of time machine," switches all over the dash, in the ceiling and in between the seats. I flipped them with satisfaction and drifted along the broken center line, which I have to admit I was eating up again, wheels lit up like a DeLorean DC-12, nearly overshooting J's Motel again. But the lights in Room 108 were out and Daryl and Dee were nowhere to be found. I left the apparatus steaming in the lot and slipped through the shadows. After all the thing was hot and the CSPD were thought quick to the scene of the thief.

Though I had no evidence of this at the time, I wouldn't take my chances. I had plans. I felt for the flier for the show later, still in my back pocket. Every time I looked at it, the line-up was rearranged and the design changed before my eyes, like many things in front of me of late. Standing in front of the toy rack at 7-11, for instance, it was suddenly clear to me.

The hints of Dee's devices surrounded me. I saw with utter clarity behind the choices on the shelves of this emporium of goods and retinal color on the Cache la Poudre corner. Those drugs of hers WERE real, but only for the right person at the right time, the right type of Silly Putty or the mints with the jokes about the mdma, the stillborn circus animal cookie overloaded with sprinkles and the trick cards, the red plastic piece for the soda crackers and Velveeta and maybe two books of magic matches. I'd just write a check for all this stuff the tender-footed Dee planted and have the time of my life, and in my hands adding the right other stuff in lieu of the ordeal at the club later. Perfect. Check, check, check.

Stradivarius sung murder, pockets crammed with concentrated kind butterscotches and blue raspberry keef suckers, rolls in his Smarties and boomers in his caramels, candy junkie mime bending the wood with his mind, choking on strawberry cough in the mauve Halls, thumbing through his five colored acid packed Fantasias with their gold tips. I'm telling you, never had time and space collapsed so as to land on the tip of my little finger. The sphinx moth on the glass door ushered me to the street, paddling my chalky red ball and cracking an Orange Crush.

I considered for a moment the electric Kool-Aid acid test and the metallic taste in my mouth while dumping out the Cracker Jacks for the surprise when I was reminded of the Onion Flavored Crow Joke. Suddenly I was in perfect step with another youngster, dressed appropriately (though naively) in a black overcoat and army boots two sizes the larger.

"Have you ever heard the one about Foxy Brown and the chicken shit? Creepinlikacrowdroppinturdsonyourladybirds-Fuckwhatwasitinthetrunkhumpinfoxybrownonabumpinsub-onourwaytosixflagssmokinpurplebu…"

SMACK! A cold pain shot through my nose as my head whipped back before I could knock out the punch line. I felt the blood's warmth down my throat, then on my face.

"Damn. Fuck, I guess I never will doubt you were real dude." I refolded and tied my now soaked handkerchief around my head and spit a puddle of blood on the curb.

"You're coming, right?" I said, looking over the tip of my nose at my sullen assaulter.

★

The blood from my nose was but a cold spot at the center of my forehead when we descended into the underground venue. At the bar I smoked two green cigarettes, one lit with a mushroom match planted by the Double-Eagle Casino the other with a blue match newly put out by the illuminati sub-organization "Camel." I made my rounds slinging my corner-store drugs at wholesale prices. For him a crunchy mint, for her a purple Skittle. But ideas of petty crime and sugary drug deals soon fell away in favor of more nuanced occupation in a world increasingly my own.

Clockwise around the club, wood floors turned into oily green concrete, the catwalk held by a nine-high blackened iron rail led to the sliding metal door with the pulley wheels, four-inches thick once sealing cadavers cold or so the story goes, the view of the dance floor twenty shoulders wide, where elbows have touched for decades of after-parties, eyes laid down on the animated roughage of the dream.

My first French kiss in this corner right here: on top of it all, twelve feet down on a wood square, touched with black light caught in arms-length glass tubes, a disco ball that has set many a mood, dancing while fumbling with my broken phone. Maps in its circuits I cracked the code, blue tooth remote control, tongue between my teeth glowing yellow green, eyes lit up ultramarine stars, subs blowing bursts of bass breeze on the face of a disc jockey ghost. The system was hacked, whiz kid unbending another row of the dead for the fatherland.

"I was just on my way out," I said at a urinal to the bouncer next to me, when he demanded to look in my candy boxes, holding now only three Smarties and two tablets of Lithium. I was escorted up the stairs and into the cold late winter night, past one inebriated clubber after the other, my hair sash hardened crimson around my head. It must have been below zero.

Besides me, there was only one man on the streets who had yet to find shelter. He followed me almost the whole mile to Louis's before he overtook me. He was one of those Indian wanderers always around when you start noticing, this one easily spotted in the baby blue down jacket he wore summer and winter.

I took in the unmistakable smell of a Black and Mild as he approached my heels. A full minute passed before I caught on to his train of thought, which had departed from its station years ago. I gathered that he worked for N.O.R.A.D. and was here to install a nanochip in my head.

"It's invisible," he said, waving his hand by my ear.

He joined me for a blue cigarette on Louis's back patio. It was as though there was not a sound left in the whole world, like every note on earth had been frozen in thin air. Maybe the air itself was gone, and there were only a few white queens sparking as they drifted to the tips of the grass. We made this so easy for each other; we had a moment to collect ourselves, to take the stillness into our hearts.

Louis was gone for the night, in all likelihood to get away from me and my masquerades. My knife-hand burned on its way through the screen. I used to live here after all, that window never locked easily, and I had nowhere else to go. I fell into deep sleep buried in his blankets.

14

Commitment

Kathy

Max sat on the washing machine while I leaned against the dryer trying to explain in a graceful way that I thought he was going crazy again. It was January and only eight months since he'd graduated. He'd been in a holding pattern since then, working in a nursing home and living at home, neither of which he planned to continue for long. He was having difficulty figuring out how to proceed with his life. I knew he'd stopped taking his Lithium. He was always on the move.

"I'm worried, Matty."

"I'm fine, better than fine."

"You're going to end up in the hospital."

"I'm okay. I'm sleeping and eating well."

"You've said that before, Matty. We need to talk about this."

"We don't need to talk. I'm fine." He left with Louis and I didn't see him for several days.

I knew about all the reasons people stopped their meds—the desire to feel the elation that comes with mania, the feeling that they aren't sick after all, the side effects. "Mania is the seductress of mental disorders," wrote psychiatrist E. Fuller Torrey in *Surviving Manic Depression*, "the psychiatric Siren calling to the passing Ulysses of the world, encouraging them to put away their Lithium and enjoy, enjoy, enjoy." Why wouldn't one want to re-experience the boundless energy, the intensity, the infinite capacity to understand the universe and the confidence to direct it?

Many believe that they can do without medication once they are stable. After all, how many of us have stopped our antibiotics too soon because we no longer suffer from symptoms? And it's not surprising that some find that the benefits of psychiatric medications don't outweigh the costs—the hand tremors, weight gain, headache, nausea, drowsiness, impaired memory and concentration, the hypothyroidism, seizures, increased risk for diabetes and cardiovascular disease.

Max complained that the Lithium was numbing and he wanted to feel alive. Today he believed he was savvy enough to manage his moods and keep the mania from spiraling out of control. But soon he stopped coming home altogether. He slept on Louis's couch and wandered the streets of Colorado Springs. Sometimes I was able to catch up with him. We argued on the way to my office where I would give him a massage, but the quarrel got left at the door. I ran my fingers along his spine and up to his shoulders, kneading a plane of tight knots.

His muscles relaxed and I felt him cry. Max had been tightly strung for days now. The contact between my hand and his skin brought us together in ways that talking couldn't.

We could be close then—I could nurture and he could accept it because it wasn't about anything but caring and healing, not interfering. An hour later, he left and I didn't see or speak to him again for days.

I was desperately hoping he'd keep an appointment with his psychiatrist. So Ron and I drove the streets of Colorado Springs looking for him in places he hung out, all on the one block we understood he practically lived. He was not among the smokers perched on the edge of a dead flowerbed outside his preferred cafe, or among the faces we searched at Poor Richard's Feed and Read, not at Tony's, his bar of choice.

"Do you know a guy named Max?" I asked the bartender. "Twenty-three, six-two, brown hair, beard, good-looking" Ron added.

The bartender hesitated, unsure about how to respond to two strangers looking for one of his customers.

"He's our son. He's not doing well," I explained.

"Yeah," he said, having noticed the problem that was Max. "He hasn't been around today. I'll call you if he comes in." He handed us a bar napkin and I jotted down our cell number.

We walked through Acacia Park, looking for him in the faces of the drunk and indigent stretched out on picnic tables and benches. We drove through the Marion House parking lot, where the homeless waited for the soup kitchen to open, then to the Red Cross Shelter. No one there knew him. At a loss, we were trying to figure out what else we could do when the cell phone rang.

"Max just came in. He's sitting here right now." It was the bartender at Tony's.

Max wasn't at all surprised when we walked in five minutes later. It was as normal as the beer sitting in front of him and the fact that he was with some guy he introduced as Travis who looked forty and high out of his mind. The bartender nodded and ambled off to the end of the bar, knowing he didn't want to be involved in this conversation. Ron and I sat on the two empty stools beside Max, trying to figure out what to do now that we'd found him.

If it had been up to Ron, he would never have started this journey in the first place. He knew futility when he saw it. But I'd sought reassurance in knowing that Max was still breathing. Of course any mention of hospitalization would have sent him straight out the door and he was certainly not coming with us. After having spent hours searching for him, all we could do was remind him that he had a doctor's appointment in an hour. He reluctantly agreed to meet us there and we could only hope that he actually would.

When Ron and I got to the psychiatrist's office, the doctor was at his desk, jotting notes on a legal pad. Max had been seeing him during summers and Christmas breaks for the last four years. He had managed Max's medication over the phone when Max was in school in Iowa. Nothing ever seemed to alarm him. I suppose one becomes accustomed to all the parental angst and patient crises. He listened quietly as we detailed Max's behavior of late and asked if he could find a way to admit him to the hospital.

"I'll evaluate him when he gets here," he said dryly.

I was relieved when Max walked in, sure he'd decide he had other priorities. But after fifteen minutes with the doctor, he stormed out of the office, gave me a look that cut me in half, and fled out to the street.

"He's not going to go willingly and I can't force him," the doctor explained to us. "He doesn't meet the criteria for a 72 hour hold." His hands were tied by the laws for commitment. His only choice would have been to resort to the police, a step nobody was ready for.

"I've given Max a prescription for Lamictal, and we've made another appointment for Monday."

Some families resort to lies to get their loved ones hospitalized, testifying that they've been threatened or that they found suicide notes, breaching any trust in their relationships in hopes of saving the lives of their suffering daughters or brothers. The current laws in most states require that there be proof that one is "dangerous to oneself or others" and the Supreme Court has ruled it unconstitutional to commit someone against his will without this proof.

As a result, people are protected from being wrongly committed by unscrupulous relatives or doctors who could once hospitalize patients with just a signature. Civil liberties must be protected; patients should have the right to make their own decisions about treatment whenever possible. But the criteria for commitment simply don't work when situations become dire and the illness takes away any capacity for rationality. Families who watch their loved ones deteriorate can't get help until the "proof" of life threatening risk presents itself and then it's often too late.

Max was standing outside on the sidewalk, smoking when we came out of the doctor's office. He was furious at my interference. "I can't stand to look at her," he said to Ron. I'd never seen such intensity behind his eyes. He really did hate me. I was overbearing and overprotective. The more I'd interfered, the more conflict I'd caused between us. But was I simply to step away and wait? Yet none of my interventions had made a bit of difference anyway. Max would disappear again.

★

Two days later, I sat at the kitchen table alone watching snow drop off the ponderosas that surround our house. The only sound was water trickling off the eves and down the gutters. The house shuddered as a sudden wind gusted across the hillside. The weatherman predicted another storm.

I should have been writing. I'd signed a three book contract with Penguin. Now I had deadlines. They wanted a new book every year. But my fingers had not touched the keyboard for weeks. I was just waiting beside the phone again. It was fruitless to try to contact Max. Even if I knew where he was, there was nothing left to say. Lost in mania, strangers had become his companions. Even Louis was regularly left behind. Sooner or later, I would get a call, probably from a cop, or from Max, his one call from jail.

He might have been arrested for any number of offenses—panhandling, loitering, public urination, smoking weed on a downtown corner. He could decide to stretch a line of cocaine across the bar at Tony's, roll up a dollar bill, and hand it to whomever might be sitting next to him. He could choose the wrong person to share his thoughts with about 'the situation" of the day. Someone who wouldn't put up with a total stranger in his face.

I tried to focus on the here and now, but I knew the phone would ring eventually and it was all I could think about. When it did, I'd need to get to the jail to insist that the sheriff take him to the hospital to argue for commitment. I was already sure he was in solitary confinement, bleeding internally and starving to death.

When the phone finally did ring, it was Louis. Max had been sleeping on his couch off and on for a week, coming and going as he pleased. But in the past couple of days, things had gotten hard for Louis. He couldn't keep up with the pace. Max was knocking on his door at all hours of the night, sometimes with people Louis had never met before, outsiders, vagabonds and the homeless. Louis was reaching out for help from me.

"Oh Louis, I just don't know what to tell you. You know that Max won't talk to us. Maybe you can tell him how hard things have become for you." I wanted to beg him not to kick Max out, but we were past that.

I awoke that night, scared and confused. It was three in the morning and my husband's side of the bed was empty. My stomach dropped for a second before I remembered that he was teaching in Belize. Little by little my nightmare came back to me: A man had called and wanted money. He had Max and if I didn't come up with the cash, he wouldn't let Max go. In the twists of the dream, Jessi was only ten and scared for her brother. She was standing beside me whimpering and I couldn't hear the man on the phone.

I thought that Max must be manic and I had to find him, but the man wouldn't tell me where he was or where to take the money. The next morning Max's psychiatrist called to tell me Max had missed his appointment.

15

The Lighthouse

Max

I had no money, but was sure Michelle's would take a bad check for a dinner for one, so I sat myself at a booth in the back.

I tried to relax and appear as though I belonged among the citizens of Colorado Springs out for a wholesome meal, wondering to myself how many banana splits I had eaten in the safe haven of this diner tucked behind a storefront of homemade candies, where many of my childhood rites of passage were celebrated: graduating fourth grade, my mediocre performance finale in *The Taming of the Shrew*, when I forgot my most important line, my first and only viola recital with the youth symphony when I accidentally switched my sheet music with a cello player just before we took the stage. I remember I used to order chicken fingers, so I tell the teenage waitress that's what I'll have.

"And coffee."

I sat and waited for the delivery of my food, fiddling with the paring knife I had swiped from Louis and brought with me everywhere, punching holes with its point in the tops of all the creamers, as I looked around at the families celebrating their own rites of passage. Flecks of white splattered the red nylon cushions while the patrons returned my gaze with what could only be a look of grave concern, an expression I had become quite familiar with of late. A worrisome father changed places with his little girl to place himself between her and me.

Excuse me, excuse me, but I am tired, young, and destitute. I've been on the street all day and didn't sit down once. Overworked and underpaid, I smell like shit. And it's for your children that I'm working YOU UNGRATEFUL SLOUCH! Worked to a fever pitch in fact. Keyed up in the park, tin soldier on the march, sifting for chards of plastic and broken glass, eating it with cinnamon and brass crosses. Raw beef around the fondue flame, I took the malady for myself. *That would have been your baby, but it wasn't. Lips parched like a charred asshole, I twisted my harried tongue into a useful thing, a numb thing, a dead thing. I am still gagging, watch me.*

"WATCH ME!" *Don't fret old man! I sold your stamp collection, I spent your buffalo head nickels and your two dollar bills. We were ripped off. You knew that. And now you're going to call me a crook?*

Stabbing the breaded chicken and squeezing the innards out of the fries, the smell of Old Spice swirled into bacon. *Five O, Five O.*

"Please put down the knife sir, we'd like to talk to you outside."

"It's not mine. I mean the blood is, not the knife."

"We can make this easy or we can make a scene."

I shook my head and laughed as he spread his feet, keeping his thumb on his nightstick, while his partner cuffed me, removing the knife from my hand with no unnecessary drama. The chip installed by the Indian in the blue jacket would make difficult a complete overhaul by the crude method of the CSPD, or so I thought to myself as they dragged me out by the chain, my limp body sweeping the hard candy aisle, past the colossal jaw breakers and ribboned lollypops, giant velvet hearts strewn around red satin tablecloths, little teddy bears clutching foiled chocolate roses.

Outside they drew me to my feet. I had no wallet, no I.D. Just a bunch of trash in my pocket.

"Are you kidding?" I said to them through the twelve holes in the Plexi divider of their cruiser, "I've lived here longer than you. Everyone knows me. Ask anyone if I'm from around here. They'll tell you I have a serious mental condition known as bipolar disorder, and I grew up right up the street."

Desperate and chained, I gambled they'd take my "get out of jail free" card, but there was really no telling what they had planned for me. I could only hope they were already under the new jurisdiction and would act accordingly, though I had my concerns about the rising interest in cleaning up the streets of the "hopeless youth." I was for the first time a little nervous in the isolation of this room I now found myself occupying and about Officer Frederick's insistence that he never leave my side.

"You know this is a goddamn hospital for cancer patients and broken legs, right?" They had taken me to Memorial Hospital, where I found myself in an empty white room lined with burgundy chairs and an issue of *Time* featuring man of the year Rudi Giuliani. It was difficult to say what this meant for me, but the austerity, bleakness, and low ceiling had me feeling uneasy, and the cat scanners and heavy ray-emitting equipment were hindering the transactions of the nanochip.

"I don't really have to piss, and not in that little cup, are you kidding? This is a joke right? I get it. Well, if I'm serving two gods you'll let me know, because damn it if I haven't got another engagement right now."

I was what you call a noncompliant patient, strapped spread-eagle across a hospital bed. A cop stared wildly at me, wedged as he was between me and the heart monitor, himself growing maniacal as his crotch took another blow from the limited play of my right fist bound with a leather strap. Two nurses held my legs down flat against the bed, hooking their hands over my thighs above the knee, while a third struggled to immobilize my left arm long enough to plunge the I.V. into my bulging vein, which he finally accomplished only to send the hoped for blood all over his spotless mint green pajamas, while a fourth cut my pants up the seam with a pair of industrial scissors.

Now, a fifth ripped off my pants and installed the catheter. The feeling that shot to my brain was one that perhaps can only be appreciated by the most sympathetic ear, the most horrific synchrony of extreme pleasure and extreme pain, a feeling that I can now only associate with eternal damnation. My urethra was forced around the tube and the siphon maneuvered up the length of my shaft as I experienced the most wretched orgasm an animal could possibly endure and come out alive.

But the drugs relaxed me as I was pushed into the white chamber, the chair tipping back on its own. A nurse swiftly prepared the six-inch lumbar needle that would soon puncture my spinal cord between vertebrae L3 and L4, a pair of gloved hands turning my bones on their side, the cold steel protruding from my back finally doing me the favor of fissuring me from this nightmare.

★

It was pitch black, and I could have been lying anywhere. In my childhood bedroom or my freshman dorm, one of my father's many houses, in the guestroom with the thin red bedspread, or in the basement curled up on the corduroy loveseat in the net of a white knit blanket. Or I was in a room I had yet to step foot in, with the wife I hadn't met yet curled around my hips. My children were in their rooms and my alarm was set. The dog was whimpering by the parakeet cage, and the sky was just starting to feel the sun.

Maybe the blue tie today, eggs today, don't forget such and such and so forth, your bus pass, your anniversary, the energy bill. Or I was in my grave, bent slightly at the knee, fingers tucked in the silk, thinking about what I did while I was alive, trying to assure myself I did the right things, that all of it was as real as I said it was. There was nobody there to humor me, or hint somehow that the whole thing was a joke. No cat to rub its back, or pen to write it out. No plans, no projects, not a single sign of light, no image in the cavern of my eye. No present, no future, no proof.

But I was a cruel joke that never seemed to get old. A nauseating pain settled in just behind my right eye, pounding sharp and dull aches winding together and flowing from my skull then down my back, where my muscles locked around this distinct tingling that induced a steadily ascending anxiety until the sensation turned all other pain into its memory. I was praying, *I mean praying* that this was a dream, and I would wake up any second, or otherwise that I was on my deathbed. Just let it be over quickly, anything that would put me to rest sooner than the ambivalent hand of God or the slipshod furies of human conflict.

I got to my feet so as not to complicate this hell with a pool of urine. But now that my attention had been drawn there, a second and totally other suite of pain arose. Bent over in a hospital bib, dark yellow shards of glass invaded my gut with an unthinkable heat, a thousand daggers stirred and twisted from my battered lover's piece, my buckling knees leaning me unsteadily over the sink. I was nearly laughing to myself (whatever wretch that happened to be) but if hell were to ban laughter this would've been the way. The agony that followed in my center reached out to the outermost moments of my limbs, while my head pounded its relentless drum, a series of six dry heaves finally brought me to my knees.

I pulled myself up again, because it was all I could do. Hands feeling through sunspots in a near blackout, with the stride of a ninety-year old I shuffled toward the glowing seams. I open the door to a blast of light, raising my arm to block its knives. I felt my legs buckle again but someone grasped my elbow and turned me tripping over my feet and back into the dark, gently laying me down and covering me with a lead vest.

★

I was at "The Lighthouse." The name was all I knew about the place for the first few days of my stay. I listened to Peoples Court marathons on a nearly broken TV attached to the ceiling by a thick metal bar, hiding my face beneath the

chairs in the diffused fluorescent light under the shade of the
seats. It was here that I endured the entirety of my semicon-
scious day as Judge Wopner gave his stern final judgments
and elaborated his moral grounds, my abdomen convulsing
whenever some nerve impulse set off a false signal of re-
maining energy or internal contents. I assumed they pulled
my body from the trash, and that the people who brought
me back to life were there. I could only hope they had good
intentions but was never consulted about a treatment plan. I
obviously had no choice in the matter, or in their thankfully
limited care of aspirin.

That night, late, I woke staring up at the bottom of my
chair to a commotion at the nurse's desk. Two new admit-
tants made a loud entrance. They went out to the smoking
alcove and lit up a pair of Camel straights, while I fought to
my feet and limped out to them. One was a native who called
himself Black Fox, the other a tall white guy with a mustache
who said he was a horse trader, both with manic tempera-
ments, and more importantly cigarettes.

"You pick up a wild horse, and then you go from one
place to the next, trading for a better and better horse, all the
way across the country," said the horse-trader.

"With three horses each," I muttered back, nauseated, but
with a sign of life from the buzz of bright tobacco.

"Yes. We will all go," said the Indian.

The next day, the three of us were sitting at the one and
only table, rolling a tin of Drum into hundreds of cigarettes.
The nurses didn't even know who I was, which was just as
well. The details of my identity didn't matter if I wasn't coming back out the other side, which seemed as likely as ever, as
I still could not eat. All the blood had drained from my face;
very possibly I was already dead.

"You should just put me back where you found me," I said when the attendant brought me an ibuprofen. Black Fox got up and poured me some water from the spout of the yellow igloo on the counter. I glanced into the paper cup. In it, floating, was a tiny square of paper picturing two red cherries, stems connected together like the slot machine icon. I took a sip, drooling as I lifted it from my tongue. The Indian darted me a look I took to mean, "you better, you little shit." and so quick enough I put the scrap back in my mouth.

"He knows better than I do," said the horse-trader. I thought about what this meant long enough to get up and stumble to the hallway bathroom, before I hit the toilet and vomit sprayed from all corners of my being. Yellow, red, green, finally black poured from my mouth, my head pounding between heaves, each convulsion spurting spinal fluid into the empty crevices of my body. When there was nothing left in me, I expelled the stale air from my empty and diseased gut, an exorcism of demons that echoed through an eternity. I finally passed out on the bathroom floor, feeling like someone just saved my life, for whatever the fuck it was worth.

16

You Better

Kathy

Max was on a 72-hour hold at the Lighthouse, a state-funded holding facility for detox and the mentally ill in crisis. I should have been grateful that the police took him to Memorial Hospital and not to jail after they arrested him. But at the hospital, he'd already been tied down, tranquillized, and given every test in the book, including a spinal tap to rule out meningitis.

When I got there, Max was sitting at a table in the lounge with his head in his arms. A social worker ushered us into his office. I was finding it hard to focus over the cement truck driving around inside my head, and I could see the pain in Max's face too. In spite of everything, he didn't want to be admitted to the psychiatric hospital where he could get real treatment, which did not occur here at the crisis center, where they could not administer medicine.

But with a call to Max's psychiatrist, arrangements were

made. An hour later, I waited in the hospital lobby while the admissions officer interviewed Max. Someday, I hoped I'd learn to handle crisis better than I had until now. I had to find a way to remove myself, let the chips fall a little. I was sitting with my eyes closed contemplating my mistakes of the past few weeks when the admissions officer appeared.

"I'm afraid we can't admit Max. He doesn't meet the criteria."

"What do you mean?" After all of this—his arrest, an ambulance to Memorial Hospital, the crisis center, the psychiatrist's recommendation, how could they possibly refuse? "What are you saying? His doctor wants him admitted! He's here voluntarily! He doesn't need to meet the criteria!"

"It's the insurance."

Of course. "If you don't admit him, he's going to end up hurt or worse. Are you willing to take responsibility for what happens?" By five, Max had his own room on the adult unit.

The next day I was back at the hospital with clean clothes for Max, who was still wearing the clothes he'd been arrested in. His wallet and backpack were gone along with any indication of his identity. He was sitting on a mattress in the hall and on "yellow," meaning he was high risk and they wanted him sleeping where they could see him.

The psych unit doctor was talking with Max when I arrived the following afternoon. I pulled a chair over and listened. I was trying to back off a little, but I knew that Max needed an advocate. When their conversation ebbed, I asked the doctor to develop a plan with Max before he was released so that he didn't end up back out on the street with no place to live and no medicine. I was relieved when Max nodded in agreement.

When I visited the hospital on the ninth day of his stay, I

was given a copy of a letter that the doctor had just received:

"Your request has been reviewed by our Behavioral Health Physician and authorization has been denied because the patient is not at imminent risk and does not require a secure 24-hour psychiatric setting. This decision is based on the Patient Placement Guidelines." They say they are in no way "seeking to influence clinical decisions or dictate treatment options." But they aren't paying. The doctor had already signed the release.

His outpatient plan involved only an appointment with his psychiatrist, the assumption being that Max would come home with me and I would take care of things from there. Max had been on medication for nine days and was leaving with a bag of pills. That was it—he was supposed to go from utter psychosis to functioning citizen in a matter of days.

★

I'd piled two stacks of mail on the counter. The biggest stack was bounced check notices— from the Sinclair station, Hathaway's Tobacconist, Boulder Street Café. Most were for five or six dollars with bank fines that had accrued to the tune of some $600. A collection company had already sent a letter trying to recoup Max's $3.62 check to 7-11 and an extra $100 in collection fees.

The other pile comprised three bench warrants. In Max's room, I unfolded a crumpled paper, an Appearance Bond. The offense was shoplifting and it indicated he was released on "personal recognizance." On the back in red marker, Max had scrawled:

1: BIG g. MAR 1.
2: ⌗
3: CLOUDY
SUNSET

Max wasn't thinking about the consequences of failing to appear in court on the designated date, a day that had long passed. It was just another piece of paper about a reality he was no longer a part of.

He had been out of the hospital for two days and came home periodically but wouldn't stay the night. Max was not what you would call, "on the road to recovery." Jessi and I spoke every night. She was my sounding board and ally. In the middle of her second year of medical school, she explained Max's situation to her professors and was granted a short leave to come home.

The day she arrived, Max came home to spend time with his sister. That night we cooked together as the tension in the kitchen grew. Max was manic and edgy, insistent that he knew exactly how the salmon should be prepared. I'd learned the futility of arguing with the manic Max. But Jessi tends toward logic and analysis and her response was sisterly impatience. She was brought to tears as she tried to break through the impenetrable wall around her brother. Somehow we managed to get through the meal and then Max took off.

As the days passed, Jessi and I talked about what we thought was best for Max. Maybe he should apply to do an MFA in art, maybe he should stay here for a while where he's got a support system. We agreed that living in Colorado Springs was a bad idea—too many dead ends and people his age going nowhere. But Max's plans changed hourly--an apartment in town, making a living selling his art, a quick road trip east. It was absurd, our notion that we had any control or influence over the matter.

Max was mostly absent, preoccupied with strangers in town again. He never made it back for dinner the next night. We tracked him down the following day, and Jessi got caught up in Max's adventures while I was at work with a full schedule of massages. When I pulled up in front the Poor Richard's Restaurant later, he was kneeling on the sidewalk in a jumble of art, screwing a frame together. Seemingly he'd talked the owner of the restaurant into hanging some of the paintings of Long Island that he'd done at the New York Studio School. Jessi was trying to clear a path through the debris for pedestrians winding their way through the confusion.

"There was no way I could help," she said when we got into the car. "I don't know if putting his art in the restaurant is okay with the owner or what's going on. I didn't know what to do."

"I don't know what to do either."

A couple of days later, Jessi had to return to school. "I'm sorry I have to leave, Mom," she said, lifting her suitcase out of the trunk in front of the airport. "I'm worried about you."

"Don't worry, I'll be fine." I knew she was crying as she dragged her suitcase inside. On the way out of the airport, I swerved into the other lane as I searched the car for a tissue to swipe at my dripping nose. The guy on my left leaned on his horn and sped by, giving me the finger.

★

On the night before Valentine's Day, I attended a mental

health forum organized by several non-profits in the community. I wasn't exactly sure where I fit in and contemplated leaving when a woman recognized my discomfort and asked me to join her discussion group. Gayle introduced herself as the coordinator of a program called Family-to-Family and the mother of a son with bipolar disorder.

Others joined us, a woman with a sister and parents with a son, both with paranoid schizophrenia, a wife whose husband suffered from PTSD. And me, mother of a son with Bipolar I. Gayle began by telling us about her son, thirty-eight, working, and on his own. Others followed with one painful story after another, stories about crisis, destruction, fear. The ones we loved were no longer the people we had always known. I told them that Max was out on the street somewhere, delusional and fully lost in his imaginary world.

As the meeting broke up, Gayle walked me to the door and handed me a pamphlet about her organization, the National Alliance on Mental Illness, which she called NAMI. For a while inside I felt less lonely, relieved to be talking with people who knew what it meant to cope with mental illness, people who were willing to listen and help each other. But out in the dark, I recalled the look in Gayle's eyes—experience and empathy, but also deeply buried grief.

The next day the police called. "We've got Max Maddox in our squad car down on Tejon Street. The charge is panhandling but he's confused and obviously in trouble. He said you're his mother."

"Would you take him to Cedar Springs Hospital?" I pleaded. "I'll come right away and meet you there." I was relieved when they agreed. I knew how this could have gone. I assumed they had discovered several warrants for his arrest. They could have taken him to jail for not appearing in court.

Our jails are filled with those who suffer from some form of mental illness. The sheriff in Colorado Springs has said he runs the largest mental-health care facility in the county. Some twenty-five percent of the inmates in the jail have serious mental illness, though that number reflects only those who have been diagnosed. I learned of one inmate who had been in and out of the jail some sixty times for minor infractions—public urination, trespassing, soliciting, shoplifting. He didn't have an address to which the warrants could go and would never be able to make a court appearance anyway due to the severity of his condition. He'd spend a few months in jail, where he began to stabilize on medication. When he was released, he was given a week's worth of medication and an appointment at the mental health clinic. He'd lose his pills, sleep in the park, eat at the soup kitchen, had no way to get to his appointment, and was psychotic in a matter of weeks. Once again he'd be jailed and the cycle began all over.

Not long ago, I'd read a letter in a mental health newsletter written to the County District Attorney. It was from a parent whose mentally ill son was caught in the loop of the local judicial system. Initially, he was picked up for driving without insurance. He missed his court date, and his psychiatrist at the VA wrote the courts to explain it was due to his illness, not any criminal intent. Then he missed another hearing, was arrested for failure to appear, and jailed.

"Where is the justice," the parent wrote, "that would allow the prosecution of a person with certified mental illness over a traffic violation? Please find a way to settle this without totally destroying my son."

Max was admitted to the hospital again. By then I knew where to find the best parking places and had learned to ignore all the signage about visiting hours, bringing food onto the unit, and all the other myriad instructions. I'd also learned my way around the courthouse, where I went before the judge and explained why my son was not present and why he had panhandled, shoplifted, and missed court dates. It was agreed that the charges would be dropped as long as Max stayed out of trouble for a year and got treatment, evidenced by reports sent from his doctor and the therapist. Given what had happened over the months, I didn't know whether Max would be able to stay clear of the law but the only reasonable choice was to agree.

Max was again released from the hospital on the ninth day, which I figured was once more decided by the magic formula outlined in the insurance "Patient Placement Guidelines." We were handed the customary brown bag of samples on our way out.

I knew Max wouldn't come home, so I decided to help him find an apartment and paid the rent. Psychologists might call it "enabling," but I couldn't leave him with nothing. Some say that you've got to let those with mental illness bottom out. I was not ready to accept that. It felt like punishment to me, revenge against Max for having this illness.

We found a basement apartment that I thought was too dark, but Max thought was just fine. We dragged a mattress from our house and found an old table and a couple of chairs. I brought him sheets and towels, dented pots and pans, plates, and mismatched silverware from Goodwill. I stocked the refrigerator and cupboards. He didn't seem at the point that he could face all this outside the hospital, but together we placed his pill bottles in a neat row in the medicine cabinet—Lithium, Abilify, and Xanax.

Ron had returned from Belize and checked on Max every day after he finished teaching and I stopped by between massages. Sometimes he was working on a drawing or lying in bed with his headset on, and sometimes he was gone. Then one afternoon when I pulled up in front of his apartment, the entire neighborhood was being treated to the bass booming from his stereo. An eviction notice demanded he move out immediately. The door was wide open and Max was gone.

I found him outside Poor Richard's Restaurant drawing a tiny figure on the corner of the window with paint markers. We went inside for lunch because I didn't know how else to keep him near except by sitting over food, which he probably badly needed right then. Two women sat nearby, shaking their heads in judgment, expressions damning. I glared back at them, anger flashing, until they dropped their eyes to their plates.

Max finally agreed to go home with me. That evening we talked him into going back to the hospital for the third stay in two months.

★

I was at home trying to write when the social worker on Max's unit called to inform me that things were hopeless. "I'm sorry to tell you this," she said without preamble, "but Max is never going to get better. The doctor has changed his diagnosis to schizoaffective disorder. I'm so sorry."

Sorry? Sorry? Was she seriously telling me on the phone that my son would spend the rest of his life in and out of delusions and hallucinations, never knowing reality again, losing his family, his life? And she was sorry? I was too shattered to ask questions.

I didn't really know what this diagnosis meant except

that it was worse than bipolar disorder. I wasn't willing to accept the doctor's prognosis without question. Max had been in and out of this hospital for the past two months, weeks that he'd been tangled in a web of tranquilizers, anti-psychotics, and mood stabilizers, not to mention the trauma of the emergency room at Memorial Hospital. Even the most stable person would be delusional after what Max had been through. What would have happened if they had kept him until he recovered the first time he was admitted two months ago?

"We diagnose schizoaffective when a patient has delusions without fluctuations in mood, in other words, when not manic," the doctor said.

He didn't seem to know where bipolar disorder left off and schizoaffective disorder began, or when schizoaffective was better described as schizophrenia. The boundaries were poorly defined and elusive for an illness that played out in countless variations. It was hard to tell whether it even mattered, to treatment or anything else, which was always decided on the spot anyway.

I'd checked the DSM which said that schizoaffective disorder is grouped in the schizophrenia spectrum. It also said that this "determination can be difficult and may require longitudinal observation and multiple sources of information" and that "the prognosis for Schizoaffective Disorder is somewhat better than the prognosis for Schizophrenia, but considerably worse than the prognosis for Mood Disorders." What about the "longitudinal observation and multiple sources of information?" How long and in how many situations had this doctor observed Max?

When I sat with him in his room that night, he told me he was done. He was lying on his bed with his arm across his eyes. "But my heart will burst if I can't do this. These waking dreams." This time he was kept in the hospital for fifteen days, by far his longest stay over the course of this episode.

He moved back into the apartment thanks to an understanding landlady. After three months of mania, he became deeply depressed. He couldn't stand the sound of the clothes dryer that rumbled next door, and he told me he heard voices one night that he wasn't sure were real. He was fighting to keep himself together anyway he could. He'd perched a makeshift easel in his kitchen. One completed piece leaned against a wall and another was taking shape. But his work was more a distraction than a passion.

I stopped by constantly and stayed as long as he needed me. I continued to stock his refrigerator with more food than he could ever eat. I brought him extra blankets and a red wool rug to cover the drab carpet in his bedroom. I found myself looking for the immediate modes of potential suicide—a place to string a rope, a sharp blade. I removed all but a few Xanax from the bottle in his medicine cabinet. Every day when I knocked on his door, I was afraid he wouldn't answer. Often it seemed impossible for him to spend the night alone, so I talked him into coming home whenever I could.

All Max thought about was suicide. I had the same imperfect responses—"It's going to get better, you won't feel like this forever." I couldn't imagine how he got through each hour of each day then struggled through the next. We talked openly and I asked him for promises I didn't know whether he could keep.

★

"You better, you better, you better," the doctor told us.

"Max would be better off without insurance. You better get him on disability. You better check on Medicare. Max would be better off in the public health care system. Drop his psychiatrist. He can't live on his own. You better check into boarding houses. You better prepare for his future. You better, you better, you better."

We spent months negotiating with collection agencies, the insurance company, and with the hospital about the bills. I filled out forms and Max signed them. I researched boarding homes and found them cold and dreary. The only one that seemed at all acceptable was $3000 a month and had a twelve month waiting list. Forms were returned marked in red—"We need more information." "We need a letter from the doctor." "Sorry, your application has been denied." I slammed all of it into a drawer, refusing to believe that Max's life would turn into this.

I convinced Max that we should plead his case to his bank about the overdraft fees, now at some $850. Depressed and hopeless, Max was sure it was futile, but he didn't have the energy to resist. We sat down with a bank manager, who had never heard of bipolar disorder until this past football season. "Yeah, the Raiders offensive lineman missed the Super Bowl. Sports page says he has bipolar. "

"Jimmy Piersall and Darryl Strawberry have it too," I said, reinforcing the fact that this illness could strike anyone, even famous athletes, and that Max's diagnosis didn't mean he was a criminal. He reviewed Max's account and agreed to drop the bank charges if we covered the overdrawn checks. I handed over the money before he changed his mind.

Max was referred to Pikes Peak Mental Health where a psychiatrist saw him for five minutes each week and gave him a refill on meds. His assigned case worker stopped by to check on him periodically and took him to the center. It was never clear just what he was supposed to be doing at that place other than playing Ping-Pong with other clients. He was assigned to the Red Team but as far as I could tell the Red Team no longer existed, and pretty soon the case worker stopped showing up.

This was the system into which Max had been thrown, understaffed, underfunded, and basically underwater. We were led down dead ends and through labyrinths that took us right back to where we started. Caring people tried to help but their hands were as firmly tied as ours because few resources existed and they had to work through the red tape of an overwhelmed system. I was more discouraged than ever and now Max was clinically depressed.

17

The Cat's Meow

Max

My head was covered with blankets on a hot July evening (or was it morning?) as the sun dropped behind the Rockies (or was it rising over the plains?), my head sweating bullets on a flattened down pillow, begging for more sleep. I mean *praying* for it, like I had never prayed for anything. But I was prostrate to a god to whom I had clearly paid little mind in my life.

I had not left my bed for a full twenty-four hours. Everywhere fumed a thickening ammonia; the smell of sleep had become my smell. My eyelids wouldn't stay shut without the greatest effort, an exertion now contributing to a pounding headache, a direct line of pain between me and everything around me. I pulled the covers off my lanky frame and threw them in a pile on the floor. I stood up and felt the slosh in my head settle and my reflection on the closet door came into focus.

"Abhorrent."

I looked down at my giant white feet gripping the malted brown carpet. My body swayed forward and then back, putting forth only the slightest effort to take the axis of the upright animal. I was born with baseball bats for legs and smashed cans for knees. It suddenly occurred to me that I needed a wheelchair to get to the bathroom.

Jesus Christ, Max. My pegs painfully lifted my unsightly dogs and sent me in the direction of the john. I took a Xanax, pulled my shorts half open, freed my shriveled penis from its little curtain, and took a sad dark yellow piss in the direction of the toilet bowl, spraying urine onto the hair of my legs, while I assured myself that half a man is not a man at all.

Such a man has only one eye and one ear, and is always looking over his one shoulder. Nobody can stand him, even if they think he's sad and pathetic. You can't really blame them, though. I mean *Jesus Christ*, he's a freak of nature, the gaping wound running his length along red severed ribs. Too spineless and disgusting to hit the seas with the ship of fools. He kills every conversation in its tracks and ruins every party with the first words out of his half mouth.

"How's it going?" is all she asked. You don't have to bring everyone down. I mean, didn't you think life would go on without you? Jesus Christ, come on! It's the one thing a human being is supposed to know! I hastily opened the refrigerator. I tried not to get caught up in all the problems inside it, grabbed a half slice of pizza and stuffed it down my throat. It got stuck halfway down, and I could only hope it would choke me to death right there on the spot. But something moved me over to the sink and cupped my hand under the faucet. *Jesus Christ Max, what the fuck is wrong with you?*

Desperately I turned on the 73 Trinitron. I got three channels: Univision, QVC, and Fox. I tried not to let these limitations warp my perceptions of the world out there, but it was all I had. Right there in my bedroom, every reason to off myself: *Sabado Gigante,* a sale on rhinestone necklaces, a cat slipping down a backyard water slide, landing in the perm of a sunbathing fat lady, just as the plastic pool bursts and puts her face down right where her audience had always wanted her.

"Ya know, I had a whole weekend like that," droned Bob Saget. "It was the cat's Meeeeeooooooww!"

I yanked opened the kitchen drawer and pulled out my only knife, the dullest one my mother could dig up in her own kitchen drawer.

"Shit," I pushed off my tongue in a quick exhalation of rotten breath, the blunt piece of steel barely scratching my wrist. I considered everything I'd ever heard about the method. My dad's college girlfriend did it with a Bic razor. I couldn't believe she pulled it off. The living human skin is so resilient, so stretchy. She must have been ruthless. Getting down to the vein, that was the key, cutting up long ways, best when done in a bathtub. But I already knew I didn't have the balls for a long massacre. I can't even stand the sight of blood.

All I had was a half-gallon of bleach and a dozen bottles of pills. God, though, the stomach cramp, and there was no guarantees there. *Jesus H. Christ, you can't even take your life into your own hands, so now you'll just have to grin and bear it for the rest of your life, lying around on the flat side of your half-body, a half burden to your whole family, until you finally bleed out fifty years... what was it? Hence, fifty years hence, you old chicken shit. Why don't you just call your Mommy?*

She suggested I take a run around the block, always her last piece of advice when she wasn't yet there to hold me. This was the first time I took it, screaming my little heart out as I rounded the corner. I spread my arms for a mercy death as clouds passed and dispersed in a pink light and the world gently spun through a malignant eternity. I fell to my knees and there again it bloomed, in a swirl around the face of a gray animal the unseen released its white line, forming its name in perfect cursive.

We steal our long lives, as I would steal mine, because I was a coward too. And this is the landscape of the rest of my life, of my life with you. Soon, the unmistakable headlights of my mother's car drifted clockwise around the room, feeling along the top of my basement walls.

★

"It's a natural response to mental anguish," explained my therapist. "It's called pain displacement. I mean, you know you can't kill yourself with a knife too dull to cut a cooked potato. And besides, *you have a lot going for yourself.*"

I stared blankly at the "triangle of health" on the dry-erase board. There is nothing like outpatient treatment to set in the utter loneliness of illness.

And yet my mom was there with me still, sitting on the bed next to me in my basement cave, when I opened my acceptance letter to graduate school, the application for which she did a wonderful job.

"Thank God," she and I said in the same breath. She had ushered me back into life once again. What can I say without resorting to cliché? I can't. Really though, you don't have to bring everyone down with you. But, of course, this means not going down at all. And so there is the contract of your birth.

18

8:32

Kathy

Sarah and Tim's chairs were empty when class began one night in late September. They arrived after the break.

"David tried to kill himself," Tim barely uttered.

By now we knew that David was Tim's and Sarah's sixteen-year-old with bipolar disorder who had been suicidal for months.

"He swallowed every pill he could find in our medicine cabinet," Sarah said. "How could we have been so stupid, leaving medication around like that? He's on a seventy-two-hour hold at Cedar Springs."

Five years ago, I never imagined I would have found myself in this classroom with other families talking about suicide. I knew the risks and that all it took was one moment, but I still believed I could outrun that moment. I glanced at the clock and hoped that Max was okay at 8:32 on this Tuesday evening.

"You've got to depend on him to get through it," said one of the teachers. "You can't be there every minute." But no matter what we said or thought, the same overwhelming fear remained for us all, so we tried fruitlessly to manage our children's lives.

We were in week six of the twelve week Family-to-Family program, offered free by the National Alliance on Mental Illness (NAMI). Everyone in the room had a relative with mental illness. For many, it was the first time they had spoken openly about their experiences. As the weeks passed, we told stories about hospitalizations, financial ruin, and destroyed families. Stories of bipolar, obsessive compulsive, and borderline personality disorders, schizophrenia, depression and post-traumatic stress. These were the wives and husbands, mothers and fathers, brothers, sisters, daughters, and sons.

"He's not working," one explained. "He says he's looking for a job, but I know he's just out driving around. He's given up. I'm not sure I can stick it out anymore. I just want him to be the man I married ten years ago. Right now, it's like I'm taking care of another child. I don't want another child. I want a partner." She was contemplating divorce and this class was her last ditch effort to figure things out.

"She lost everything," said another. "Now she lives on the streets. She doesn't believe that she has schizophrenia, won't do anything to help herself, or listen to anything we tell her. All we do is argue. I can't stand to see her anymore. She's not the daughter we raised."

An older woman in the class, a retired teacher, had been taking care of her son for forty-two years. He had paranoid schizophrenia. Her adult daughter sat quietly beside her, knowing that at some point she was going to have to take over her brother's care. After so many years, her mother had accepted her son's limitations and behavior. She'd given up trying to convince him that he didn't need to duct tape the seams around bedroom windows and spray for insects. After years of experimenting with medications, she believed this was the best it was ever going to be for her son. Sometimes medication and a caring family simply couldn't help a person become what we once hoped them to be.

I told my story too. That two months ago, I had been preparing for the worst—that Max would be incapable of living on his own. I knew it was risky to look too far into the future. Before he got sick, I assumed Max would graduate from college, maybe go on to graduate school, find a fulfilling career, get married, and maybe have kids. He had already accomplished so much, but I knew his road would be harder and more complicated, and that he'd continue to follow a crooked and unconventional path.

By the end of our twelve week class, many had let their anger go and quit blaming their loved-ones. And we'd stopped blaming ourselves. We'd accepted the "new normal" of life with mental illness. We left that last night with two-inch thick binders filled with information about mental illness, about what to do in a crisis, and how to communicate, problem solve, and take care of ourselves. We'd become educated and empowered. We'd learned that recovery was possible and that we weren't as alone as we'd once thought.

★

Max worked in pastels, wall-filling pastels, five feet tall and seven feet wide collections of bold dark strokes with splashes of color depicting a classroom full of jumbled chairs and stools. They looked as though they'd move and change shape the moment your gaze strays. He was completing his first year of graduate school at the Pennsylvania Academy of Fine Art in Philadelphia and had been awarded one of two MFA Merit Scholarships. It covered his tuition while a school loan covered his living expenses which meant he could move out of his dad's small apartment next semester.

I'd spent the past year going to writing conferences, doing book signings and interviews for my first book. The second would be released in three months. I'd felt compelled to introduce the issues of mental illness in this book and did so through a new character, a heroine who had bipolar disorder and worked as a conservationist. It was the beginning of my efforts at advocacy for those with mental illness.

In April, I visited Max for a couple of days on my way to Washington D.C. to speak at a conference. Max was waiting for me at the subway when I arrived. He crushed his cigarette under his shoe and hurried toward me, smiling *that* smile. Behind us William Penn perched on the top of City Hall, the streets wrapping him in the confusion of car horns, exhaust, and rushing pedestrians.

Max grabbed my suitcase and we headed west through Love Park and past dozens of cheese steak stands billowing grease at 10 a.m. We reached the Academy on Cherry Street and took the elevator to the ninth floor, where studios were filled with half-formed figures in clay, saturated canvases, collages, objects made of castoffs from our daily lives, and pieces to which I couldn't put a name. They were small havens of work and repose, furnished with tattered couches or overstuffed chairs, reading lamps, and throw rugs.

Not Max's. His was a cacophony of disorder. Shelves were laden with boxes of pastels, tubes of acrylics, brushes captured in soup cans. Sketches were piled in a corner— buried under screwdrivers, hammers, nails, a bolt so huge I couldn't imagine why he even had it. But then I couldn't imagine what he'd do with the old telephone that laid in pieces on his drawing table next to empty coffee cups and full ashtrays. An oriental throw rug was curled at the edges, the pattern hidden under pastel dust and paint stains. An old futon resided under the huge windows that spanned an entire wall with a view of downtown. A navy blue sleeping bag was bunched up on the floor. Finished pastels graced the walls, saving the place from oblivion.

Max complained about his psychiatrist, a resident at the University of Pennsylvania Hospital. He was angry that she was always late and he'd had to wait sometimes over an hour past his appointment time. He considered it disrespectful and the relationship unbalanced. He felt as though he was simply a "case study" for the med students who frequently sat in on his appointment. Still he went once a month and he filled his prescription for Lithium.

For a long time, Max had resisted taking Lithium because it required regular blood tests to insure that the levels were not toxic but high enough to be therapeutic. He'd always had a heavy aversion to sharp needles, and Lithium had been known to cause tremors, an especially difficult side effect for an artist. But his doctor explained that it had been shown effective at lower doses without noticeable side effects, so Max had agreed to try it.

Today, thousands of people with bipolar disorder take Lithium and the American Psychiatric Association lists it as the treatment of choice in addition to the more recently developed Valproate, which is chemically manufactured and more expensive than Lithium. Found in ores and mineral waters, Lithium has a long medicinal history. Ancient Greek physicians recommended Lithium-rich mineral springs for patients suffering from mania, and later the Romans prescribed visits to the springs for their healing effects, both physical and psychological. In the nineteenth and early twentieth centuries the presence of Lithium in mineral waters made them popular in Europe and America for drinking and bathing. Even FDR soaked in the curative pools. A natural substance, Max found it more acceptable. His hands were fairly steady, so in spite of the necessary blood tests, Lithium became his drug treatment of choice.

But I knew that Max was struggling. He was at odds with his father and instead of going home to the apartment they shared, he grabbed meals near school and slept in his studio. Like the repeated patterns of a patchwork quilt, Max was being pulled out of his life again by manic depression. The day I left, we took the trolley to downtown Philly. He was on his way to school and I was headed on to Union Station. I wished a smile would light his eyes, but it never did.

On June 9th Ron and I were anchored in a harbor on Nevis, the island where Alexander Hamilton was born and where Horacio Nelson found a wife, an island of crumbling sugar mills and greenback monkeys, its peak hidden in clouds that hugged the summit. We were drifting in the harbor when the cell phone rang.

"He's okay, Mom," Jessi said, which I knew only meant that Max wasn't dead.

19

The Spirit of Transportation

Max

I felt at last calm as the train streamed east. Its embryonic rhythm brought me as close as I could to grasping the sandman's paw as the cold sun broke. But the string of insistent memories and reflections rose up again and sleep escaped me. I could almost have been dreaming, it had been three nights since my head had laid to rest. Salvation to perdition, my illness was killing me. But let me explain the insomnia.

Night 1: A sweat lodge. Bridges to the heart, a general disdain for medical science, or so I assumed. But it didn't matter, I had lost my Lithium regardless, which I needed in order to sleep. The Miqmaq splashed the hot slab, the steam flowed over his head vermillion. We put our faith in the elder, but placebo or pixie dust I was in strangeland by the time we left the ceremonies in an electric rainstorm moving swiftly over upstate New York.

Night 2: Buffalo, stark-naked in a motel on a king mattress with no blankets, confounding the sparkles in the ceiling for star maps in gold chips. Simply unable to break the boundary of waking life. Coming to terms with this, now penniless I had failed to procure more medicine.

Night 3: Earnest in my desire to burn a hole in my hand with a railroad stake jammed into the electric coil of a stove, I explained the Hegelian dialectic to my friend's younger brother, framed by our recent sweat with the Miqmaq: the flame stone, the visions, the hints of the Book of Luke, angel couples scooping up the silk; my mountainous birth was a practical secret.

My neighbor in seat C of our train car snapped at my interruptions. He looked like a Kabalistic shepherd with his groomed beard and leather-bound book.

"Where will we end up, do you know?"

"New York. Please, I'm trying to read."

"But how does it all work out?"

"PLEASE!"

Eyes heavy, drifting, I held my tongue through Rochester, Syracuse, through the Allegheny Plateau, now a mere sliver of the Atlantic Ocean. Soon the Hudson would cap off the trees of the Catskills, but for now along the tallest ridge, the ark rolled on. Within its seats, glimpse the true believers, saddened but deeply moved. It simply doesn't get old. It's the myth of the deluge.

Ahead of the storm, into the corridor to Manhattan with an envoy from the Cote-d'Ivoire. He bought me two pairs of sunglasses and a Statue of Liberty for himself.

"You know that's a pencil sharpener."

He insisted we head back toward Penn Station, likely preventing me from crossing my other half in the Big Apple. Of course it was of no concern to me, with my ideas about diamond dust and the like, the guy with the suitcase full of money and so on; moves were being made.

And so we departed to Philadelphia. I watched through the window as we rocked back and forth. I could only imagine what happened to the City. I was surprised how calm everyone was there, but I supposed it was better that way. Take your death with honor, let the water slide over you.

"This is Jersey, right?" asked my tall friend from across the aisle.

"It was," I said, "It was."

We arrived in Philadelphia long delayed and unannounced. The African had become suspicious and wouldn't lend me the three bucks for public transit. One leg of the local away from home, I spent my fourth night without sleep striding the streets under my own steam.

Walking up Broad in my new sunglasses, I had never enjoyed Philadelphia with so much satisfaction. It seemed to me so lawless, like it didn't matter what you did. I swear to you, there was never a population as fortunate as ours, that we took the only drop thousands of years could squeeze out of the universe and drank it for ourselves. And the Old World look of the whole thing, *The Spirit of Transportation*, *Angel of the Resurrection*, the utter quiet Schuylkill, scattered about, so many versions of the Reichstag rising over ashen cement eagles.

Stolen there was the *Arc de Triomph,* at its far end a bronze Ben Franklin still raged on his press. Major General John Fulton Reynolds looked Nor'east as I slipped into the lairs of City Hall, through the courtyard on a needle to south Broad upside down in the blue and pink mirage. To the echo of a horn, the faces of Calder's beasts, the holes in the world's straightest street, in the twilight of the human plight, tourists ate fettuccine, opera-connoisseurs stepped from stretch limousines, hookers were on the scene and of course the man with the tambourine, no different than me just a page of the symphony.

In the city of cathedrals, the shipwrecked dwelt in thresholds wherever they still stood. I must have taken one for my hired hand because he wore my spare shades and went on about fair trade as we walked the Avenue of the Arts like we were the only ones privy to the true *ars poetica*. We dropped in on Dirty Franks where my friend drank whatever was around and stole me someone else's beer, razorblade between my teeth like I was there for an old family feud. But the barkeep smartly asked us to make our excuse and my new friend finished his pitcher spilling half on his shirt.

We appeared at the Academy looking, well, like art students, and the guard waved us in.

Pesky temptress, the blackest night fell; a restless Aries, her perfect criminal.

"Wanna have a séance?"

"Whatever Max, it's your place." Frankincense and Myrrh, turpentine and pencil shavings on cedar, my homeless friend could have cared less that I had set a fire on the table beside him.

"What was your name again?" He was already asleep on my futon.

Dripping in blue-black under purple stars, summers passed.

★

I woke to the smiling face of Theresa (who was, to my chagrin, still married). I was simply awestruck. Of course I never thought I would see her again. But now I couldn't wait to see her to the other side. From the look in her eyes she was probably already there. My emotions for her mixed with my embrace of the beautiful day, which, after all, came after the one before. We made plans to meet later that night for a party, which sounded great to me at the time. I thought I could use a little rest and relaxation, some absinthe and whatever we were gonna get. Some weed goddammit.

"What was your name again?" My partner didn't hear me over all the noise of the business district. Gilgamesh and Hubaba we walked the streets in our dark sunglasses, intimidating the suited members of the Center City bustle. He came up with twenty bucks just by scaring nine-to-fivers on their lunch break.

No time to lose enroute to trade prints of dead presidents for human lives, a few may be lost in the wind to prime the march. Latte in my left hand, right finger in the air, I had a few things to say about the subject, from a sound proof bubble in an invisible suit I waged my grievances. To you, the citizen, to you I made my plea. To me, the future me. Feet burning on Center City streets heating pipelines through the Caspian Sea. Senator Strom Thurmond on hour twenty-four losing his place.

"GRRRRR." On the Bank One stoop, not even the guard wanted a confrontation with this pale over-caffeinated psycho, spinning circles in the revolving door just to make himself sicker. Through Love Park, sweating under GlaxoSmithKline, the incessant nine beeps and red digital readout. And into mirrors, *it was art.* Still the stone was unreduced, under a canvas curtain, there where I wrote, spilt, spoiled. Cracked. Arranged, re-arranged, deranged. It wouldn't be mine for the keeping. Or it would. Yes it would, a pastel crushed down a line on my studio wall, the handful of red pills I swallowed. Hours must have passed, but Theresa came after all.

★

"What was taking her so long, who is this Max guy and is he fucking my wife?" Theresa's abusive husband must have asked himself from his car nine floors below while he flipped through his FM favorites.

And where did I get a five-pound six-inch bolt and who cares? It just all fit together, I was once a Little League pitcher. The thought of falling was enough, a split second to picture it...BOOM! Like a shotgun, through sparkles of glass the iron cleared the air. My laptop performed its final calculation as it hit the pavement, graphite powder burst like the soul's dust on my paintings as they descended, watercolors like a flock of colorful caterpillars bounced off Cherry Street, already freshly painted yellow and purple with accents of collage. Down it all went, executor flamboyant like Galileo finally proving his theory of falling objects, until all that was left was my futon, which also had to go, even if it only fit in three pieces.

To the beat of a hurtful drum, in the midst of acts yet invisible, incomprehensible, my sweet Theresa waltzed as my paintings dropped to the pavement. *Clap clap, wake up dear lover, come back!* Unhinged herself, behind the locked studio door she screamed in the name of common sense, as the parked cars on Cherry Street got remodeled and the historic Academy Museum lost its frosted skylights, for a moment the snow globe it always longed to be.

I finally stripped naked and disposed of my clothes with particular haste, only to slice a vein on my back hand and set forth a fountain of blood pumped hot by a racing heart. Whipping my arm, I turned the walls red Pollock's as I danced with trees on blood covered feet over the chop of a black helicopter, occasioning to meet the red dot of a military rifle, special operations hovering in a hologram with its sights on a bag of bones.

The shot was clean. Right foot back, arms tucked in, braced for three quick strides and a swan dive into the lake of fire, my body strobe-lit in the short frames of my diminishing image, finishing up my work with the drop of my mucus-filled skin and hot organs splattered over my discarded life as an artist. Stopping cold at the edge of the empty frame, the breeze brushed my face as I looked over the city, my blood too thin to push me the last step. I can only assume I was still afraid to die.

20

XYZ

Kathy

Huge paintings are propped against the walls and leaning on one another. Faces, figures, animals, swaths of color
emerge out of a black background. His drawing of a boy in
a purple jacket playing a violin in what looks like a jungle is
tacked above his desk. Max told me it was inspired by a story
about an Austrian mental patient who was told by his 4th
grade teacher that he might prefer a life playing the violin in
the forest.

Stacks of paper, boxes of markers and charcoal, cuttings
from old books, sketches and half-finished drawings cover
every surface. Tackle boxes are full of found objects, waiting for their place in one of his creations. Bookshelves sag
with Pynchon, Hesse, Derrida, Habermas, Schiele, Cornell.
Every surface makes it clear that an artist works here. Max
is healthiest when he's working, happier still when his work
goes well. He sometimes paints or draws for six to ten hours

a day. He can be so focused that an entire day passes and it's dark outside before he notices. He's found ways to pay the bills without compromising his work, but has always been able to depend on his family's support. Over the years he's taught, staffed galleries, curated exhibitions, worked for a well-regarded artist who has become his mentor, and professionally photographed other artists' work. Max is striving to make a name for himself in the art world. This past summer, he fell in love and married Maria.

People with mental illness can and do succeed. They live fulfilled lives, working and developing significant relationships. They engage in the process of recovery, knowing that recovery doesn't mean cure. How do they do it? They believe in themselves. They persevere through hardship. They risk failure. They define their own life goals and design their unique paths based on their own needs, strengths, preferences, and backgrounds. They find meaning and purpose in jobs, school, volunteerism, or other endeavors.

They are supported by allies—family, friends, peers, who believe in their potential to recover, who stand by them, offering hope, support, and encouragement. Their doctors and therapists partner with them. These professionals listen rather than dictate. They offer hope rather than dismal prognoses. They allow their patients to live up to their potential and find purpose by helping them find good outpatient care and support. They support their clients in their own personal journeys.

Those who work to recover develop coping and problem solving skills, becoming their own experts, in order to identify stressors and the triggers that can lead to crises. They engage in active prevention and find personal ways of responding and coping. They maintain regular schedules, get plenty of sleep, exercise, and eat well.

They pay attention to their mood shifts, notice when anxiety rises or when an unknown voice repeats itself, and they ask themselves, "why?" Too much interaction with others, jet lag, too much noise and frenzy, the change of light with the change in the season? During difficult times, they make adjustments—take quiet walks in the park, listen to music, talk with their doctors about medication changes, pamper themselves with comfort food and naps.

Unfortunately, misperceptions about mental illness are pervasive and have serious consequences for those who struggle to recover. Negative attitudes and beliefs about mental illness lead people to fear, reject, and discriminate. The prejudice and stigma that is so entrenched in our culture set the stage for social exclusion and limited opportunity. Our misperceptions and ignorance place barriers in the way of those trying to recover.

Families can be the best advocates possible and still the ones they love can end up in prison, homeless, or worse. There's no XYZ path to healing but rather a tangle of red tape, inconsistency, and lack of treatment options that set the mentally ill up for failure. So many things can go wrong and often there are few places to turn. We need legal intercession when someone is charged with a crime so people are treated rather than jailed. We need good outpatient care, not the hit and miss care that it took us so long to piece together out of a shattered system. We need community support, strong mental health care systems, and acceptance and appreciation throughout society for people affected by mental health.

Those with mental illness and their families are working hard through grassroots organizations to institute change. They are supported by many in the mental health community. I volunteer for NAMI and I speak out about the injustices. I began by teaching the NAMI Family-to-Family class I'd taken the year before. Eventually, I directed the program, joined the board of directors, then served as president.

My work there has been my way to stand up for Max and others with mental illness. I recommend NAMI to every person who loves someone with a mental illness. There we find compassion and support and the resources to become empowered. We become advocates, telling our stories, putting a face on mental illness, and breaking down the barriers of stigma. In the process, we are transformed as we turn our pain into strength, our words into change.

Max has succeeded for many of the reasons others do. He's been scared and discouraged, but strong and determined. He believes in himself and so do those around him.

21

Real Music

Max

The Deep Rock bottle lets off its familiar bellow through the waiting room of the University of Pennsylvania Behavioral Health offices, as I pick up a *Highlights* Magazine and take my customary seat by one of those stringy plants that need absolutely no sunlight to survive. It still surprises me to see what seems like the same person every week slumped over the heavily stained chair that sits right beneath the TV proffering the latest twist of *General Hospital*, only on mute.

I try to seem involved in my reading material and mind my own business, but I can't keep my eyes from wandering, from guessing why everyone is here. How hard a twenty-eight-year old, such as me, stares at a kid's magazine might be the only hint that something is off kilter; most of those who make their appointments are the invisibly afflicted. We could be standing behind you in the grocery line, spying on your yogurt choices, blankly gaping at J-Lo's cellulite on the celebrity gossip rack, or waiting impatiently at the red light as you push your double stroller eight inches in front of our bumpers.

Frequently the most animated person in the room is a dandy in a silk suit doing his damdest to catch one of the young residents on her way past mission control. Samples and pens spilling out of his pockets, coupons for the latest and greatest, bonuses for the unsigned, he's not to be confused with one of the patients, who, on the whole, are extremely good at limiting the evidence they offer concerning their particular tick.

The waiting room music is always the same, the Musak with which we are, by now, all-too-familiar. Yes, it's that almost discounted ring, emanating beneath the chords of every pamphlet on the rack and every definitive source on the shelf, flapping the wings of the institutions that rebuild us, among them, certainly, the one at hand. It's that persistent and tedious but relentless beat, the lists of symptoms and side effects, the short-and-to-the-point anecdotes, the four-four time of recovery and relapse, the persistent quarter notes of diagnostic charts. 'Grandiosity' looms over the striving, 'self-elation' impends the celebrant, finally putting to rest our anxieties about our dreams the only way we know how: by absolving the dream itself, by snubbing *real music.*

And just like that, no more Thelonious Monk, no more of his insistent hands. No more of the nightmare of his play. Even if we can benefit from the often-harsh regimen of vitamins thrust upon us, the question of whether the mesh surrounding the mentally ill protects the sufferers themselves, or only serves to sanctify the general public and their habits, has the most ambiguous answer. So when the afflicted are offered helping hands, the intentions of their purveyors are in constant need of scrutiny. Half the time paranoid to begin with, a 'consumer' might wonder if he can trust anyone at all.

The jury is out. Clutching reason like a privilege, and deemed unable to bear witness to ourselves, the case is dismissed, we hope, as we have no defense in the prisons to which we are destined. It's unfair but it's much more than that. They can take everything. Now I want to know what's needed to live a long and prosperous life. A free life, a life from which I leave knowing the truth about myself. One where I don't die at the hand of a stranger, especially if that stranger is me.

Right around the time I get comfortable with my mark-up of "What's Wrong with This Picture," my therapist calls me into his office. The first question is always the same.

"Any change in medication?" Actually there have been a lot of changes. It's still too hot to take all four pills. And twice I thought about taking them and then forgot on the way to the sink. I called in my prescription and didn't pick it up until the next day, which caused me to miss two days because I forgot I picked it up. I went to Atlantic City with my dad where I lost a pill in the sand and one somewhere in the Tropicana.

"No change." I have come to accept that we will never be quite on the same page on the topic of taking pills. For instance, he has recommended something over-the-counter for my heartburn, but I can't bring myself to pick it off the shelf. I just can't help being suspicious, as though the conspiracy really went that far, and was really right there under our noses.

"But it works, you will never have heartburn again."

And what could be redeeming about acid-reflux? Who wants to worry about what they eat, how much coffee they ingest? I can stomach the occasional blood test and have found that my addiction to caffeine is the primary cause of the tremor in my hands, but it's never without great trepidation that I swallow my prescribed Lithium each night. Yes, there is the unquestionable allure of the manic temperament, but there is also the sense that I've been interrupted mid-sentence. I can't help but think something important is being censored, something which concerns my health. Maybe something that concerns my very destiny, but who knows? How *could* we know?

I will never be sure of the odds that led me to choose one way over another. But still I had to choose. Having failed to do my homework again, the conversation drifts to my ex-girlfriend and then to my future. It seems that uncertainty is still my greatest obstacle, though I have my doubts. Around the thirty-fifth time I look at the clock, it dawns on me that this is my graduation day from therapy.

"So how do you feel? Are you ready? I think you are."

My therapist is a full head and a half shorter than me, but he has never had trouble making me shrink. He's not "fresh off the boat," and knows I can make an argument for anything. And some part of me still thinks this is all a big test, that I could blow the whole thing and he could write me out another little appointment card, or I could open the door to find two boys-in-blue, lazily taking in the end of a soap to pass the time before they throw me in the paddy wagon.

There would be nothing to stop me from never coming back to 34th and Walnut anyway, but I know I wouldn't be able to help myself. I guess, after all, I want to be one of those invisibles. Which isn't to say that's the point of regularly staring at a stranger's narrow mustache for fifty minutes, considering whether Hitler was reborn a sweet short guy from Mumbai.

"Well, I feel good." I do feel good. Today, anyway, it seems like it could all still work out for the better, allowing for the obstacles so clearly in the way.

"And I trust your opinion." At least, I am acutely aware when I'm fooling myself in here. I'm not sure I've really created an accurate portrait of the goings-on in my mind, but I suppose that's part of the point, and he rarely steered the conversation in the direction of the imaginary. This, I have found, is finally a private affair of the mind for the clinician. My condition, when all is said and done, is a physical malady for even the psychotherapist. Illusions once repressed from the rooms of our recovery, they tell us it's finally our upturned lives that need piecing back together.

"I think I am ready." Actually I have no idea what that means, but no matter. He seems to be buying it, or at least recognize my effort to take the question seriously. I'm supposed to be writing a book about this, besides, so I've compromised my case. And what can I say, he has been a good therapist.

There are no cops hunting mental patients in the hall, just the old rigmarole. I fold up my last yellow receipt and stuff it in my pocket. I won't bother with the diagnostic chart on the back, having gotten the idea, by now, that he will never circle "In Full Remission." He is too precise for that. Besides, I'm not sure any of us within the columns really ever enjoy the luxury of being 'cured.' It would only mean that some terrible mistake was made in the first place.

Never out of the question. But when the elevator opens, where the sun strives to break through the tall blackened windows, I'm embarrassed to confess that I feel a little sentimental, walking across the lobby with an almost unbearable smile on my face, like I just won the Pulitzer or was reborn with the strength back in my weak limb. If for no other reason, I guess, than my obsession with the eleventh hour can finally depreciate back to what it was.

I push the revolving door, and the flush of street air rushes around me. The light is like a drug as it spears my eyes. The white noise of Philadelphia at noon fills my ears, and the smell of hot gristle bellowing from tin stands brings on its usual revulsion, just as though the city meant to remind me of where I am.

Of who I am.

Too early for that, I buy a sour coffee and drape my headphones over my ears, saving my last token. The walk to my art studio, where awaits the other half to this ostentatious game, is only ten blocks and the weather is exquisite. Despite the debacle here entrenched, I have a crush on this city.

I swim in her swirling marble to the tune of "Blue in Green." The anticipation is unconquerable; my future has never felt so unknown to me. In candy striped paths dance my skeletons, ambitious, animated, sparkling. *I mean Jesus Christ.* Crooked was the lie as it bestowed this gift: still hot the breeze comes at me from all sides, blowing me through a paradise.

All that sleep lost to dreams, now feel the silence of even moods. Walking on the margins, straightening out my last lines, no end to the concerns of love. Locked up in a case but still intact the map, now nothing in my grasp but this empty paper cup. Down comes the milk when fall my eyes, overflowing along my sleeve it chills my heart.

Authors' Note

The National Alliance on Mental Illness (NAMI) is a grass-roots organization founded in 1979 by parents with mentally ill children. The organization addresses the full spectrum of major mental illnesses. Local affiliates offer peer and family support groups, local information and referrals, and educational programs such as Family-to-Family, Peer-to-Peer, and In Our Own Voices, Living with Mental Illness. NAMI is a powerful voice at the local, state, and national level with more than 12,000 local affiliates spanning all 50 states, the District of Columbia, Puerto Rico, the Virgin Islands, and Canada. To find out about services, support groups, and classes in your area, or to get involved, go to www.nami.org

National Alliance on Mental Illness
3803 N Fairfax Dr., Ste 100
Arlington, VA 22203
Main: 703-525-7600
Member Services: 888-999-NAMI

Acknowledgements

Thank you to Laurie Wagner Buyer, who read the first moments of this book years ago, called them wonderful, and told us to just keep going. And to Clark Smith, for trudging through our manuscript in its infancy.

Thanks to Richard Torchia for placing his faith in Max and for his continuous encouragement and support.

Indebted gratitude to Kirby Kim who helped make this a real book.

To our family for their love and support, most especially:

Maxine Dornemann for drastically overpaying Max for yard work, her long standing and selfless sponsorship, and above all her endless and forgiving love.

Maria J. Maddox for her encouragement and invaluable editing, her elegant synopsis for the back cover, and for putting up with Max.

To Ron, whose love and constancy kept us grounded when life seemed out of control, and whose patience we have always counted on.

And deepest gratitude to Jessi, who has been with us every step of the way, loving, giving, supporting, and crying with us.

About the Authors

Kathy Brandt has published four mystery novels with Signet Books, in addition to a host of articles in nationally distributed magazines. She taught writing at the University of Colorado for ten years. She was on the Board of Directors of the National Alliance on Mental Illness in Colorado Springs (NAMI-CS) for six years and served as President for two years. In 2012 she received the NAMI National Award for her outstanding service to the organization. She is currently the NAMI-CS liaison to the Mental Health Court in Colorado Springs. Kathy also writes the Hannah Sampson Underwater Investigation Series. Kathy has a B.A. in English and an M.A. in Rhetoric. She lives in the mountains of Colorado.

Visit www.kathybrandtauthor.com

Max Maddox has a BA in philosophy from Grinnell College and an MFA from the Pennsylvania Academy of Fine Art, where he was nominated for the Joan Mitchell Award and received the Fellowship Trust Award. He has exhibited his work in galleries including The Slought Foundation, The Print Center of Philadelphia, and the Ellen Powell Tiberino Memorial Museum. He was curator at the Sun King Gallery and Pyramid Museum in Philadelphia and also assistant to artist and curator Richard Torchia, Director of Arcadia University Gallery. He now lives in Colorado where he taught at the Art Students League of Denver until 2012.

Visit www.maxmaddox.net.